Conten

Preface

Pensions Simplified has been written to make one of the most complex subjects – pensions – easy to understand and to comprehend, whilst giving the reader sufficient information to make important and vital decisions that will ensure a successful retirement.

In the past few years, the Government has been at pains to ensure a pension for all and to develop a safe pensions-savings environment, with employers to do their marketing for them. This has resulted in the much-hyped stakeholder pension scheme.

However, the general public remains deeply suspicious about pensions and their real worth. This mistrust arises from past events, and has not been helped by falling stock market prices resulting in decreasing pension fund values. The values of some funds have fallen by over 30% during 2001/2002.

Much stems from corporate mismanagement and fraud against pension funds (Maxwell); pensions mis-selling on a gross scale; the failure to deliver on annuity promises from one of the oldest and most respected pensions providers (Equitable Life); the winding down of the State Earnings Related Pension Scheme (SERPS); and the lowest annuity rates in over 40 years.

To compound this present unhealthy state of affairs, the mechanism of retiring from your fund has not only been inflexible for most, but also fraught with traps and dangers. You could lose your entire pension fund if you die too soon; the general inflexibility of annuities to give you realistic increasing income in retirement – the dangers of the misuse of income draw-down when using your pension fund as a money box up to age 75 (you could deplete your capital by then) are all areas for concern.

For those in final salary schemes, the failure of many employers to meet funding commitments and the new accounting standards requirements whereby decreases in pension scheme values are shown as a deduction against business profits will also contribute to a changing landscape as more and more final salary schemes change over to money purchase arrangements, or do not admit new members.

It is no wonder then that pension savers are sceptical, if not cynical about what the future holds for them. For one, employers are looking to cut costs, not increase them, and increasing pension contribution liabilities for employers will become unsustainable and funding will reduce, not increase, in the future.

Saving for retirement is therefore more important than ever before. People are retiring earlier and living longer. Many people can expect to live half their lifetimes in retirement in the 21st Century. With the move to equalise the state retirement age for women to age 65 (from 60) from April 2010 for ten years, the age when men retire from the state scheme, a large mass of people will be on reduced incomes and may have gaps to fill. The new state pension age will be 65 and this will affect all women born before 5th April 1955. Women born after April 1950 and before April 1955 will have a state pension age of between 60 and 65.

Certainties, like final salary schemes, are not so certain any more. For the self-employed and those employees without pension schemes, there will be a need to save even harder than ever before (to make up for falling share values and low expected annuity rates).

The major objective for most people will be to ensure a successful retirement, and a plan of action will show how best to build it.

Retirement planning is not just about pensions, but about building a savings plan that includes pensions. It is not only about what has been done or accomplished in the past, but what can be accomplished in the future.

Knowing your way around the pensions maze, avoiding the major pitfalls and traps that will cost you time as well as money and knowing how to manipulate the system can significantly increase your pensions' wealth and retirement success.

This book is about not only about how to beat the system, but also how to understand the complex issues to make it easier to accumulate pensions wealth in uncertain times.

I am fortunate enough to have Richard Bateman as co-author for many parts of this book. Richard has over 20 years of coal-face pensions experience as an independent financial adviser, helping clients with financial planning and pensions issues for families and businesses. Richard has for many years wanted to see an authoritative work that simplified the pensions process, and thereby the work of his financial planning colleagues.

Tony Granger

About the Authors

Tony Granger has been a retirement specialist and financial planner for more than 20 years. He was instrumental in forming the first Annuity Bureau to get the best open market option pension and annuity deals for clients, and has developed many new pensions products. He is the author of many publications and books, including 'How to Finance Your Retirement ' (Random House/Century), 'Wealth Strategies for Your Business' (Random House/Century), 'EIS and VCT Investors' Guide' (30 Day Publishing),and the 'Retirement Planning Workstation' (30 Day Publishing) which includes booklets on 'Annuities' 'Pensions' 'Estate Planning' and others. His latest work is 'Independent Financial Advice and Fee-Based Financial Planning'.

He has campaigned for many years for a better deal for those saving for retirement and has developed innovative retirement planning products to increase income and capital in retirement.

Tony is a member of the Institute of Financial Planning and holds the CFP, the certified financial planner certificate, as well as degrees in law and commerce. He is a past president of the Institute of Life and Pensions Advisers (Financial Planning Institute) of South Africa.

Richard Bateman is an independent financial adviser with over 20 years experience in financial planning. From his early days as 'The Man from the Pru', Richard has developed a practice as an independent financial adviser, advising clients in all aspects of retirement, pensions and investments, and has tirelessly worked for a better deal for his clients. He holds the MLIA (Dip) and involves himself in motivational and financial education matters through the Life Insurance Association (LIA), where he has been recognised as a 'Top of the Table' participant amongst the world's financial planning elite. Richard brings a simple philosophy to his work that is highly motivational for both himself and his many clients, and that is to get the best deal for his clients, whilst providing the highest level of service.

1

Pensions as Part of Retirement Planning

Retirement planning is the combination of pensions, savings and investments with the long term goal of providing tax-free cash (or tax efficient cash) as well as annual income to secure a comfortable and successful retirement.

Pensions usually play a major part in retirement planning, but are not the only savings vehicles to be considered. Whilst conventional pension funds provide a tax-free investment growth vehicle during the investment term, there are numerous choices at retirement to opt for a mixture of tax-free cash and a lower pension or annuity – which is taxable – or for the full pension fund to be used to buy pension benefits.

If you are a member of an occupational final salary pension scheme, then the size of the tax-free cash and the amount of the pension payable depends on the number of years service with your employer and the actuarial factors employed within the scheme rules such as final salary definitions, as well as additional funding to boost benefits such as AVC's or free-standing AVC's, as well as stakeholder pension benefits, for earners under £30,000 per year.

If you are a member of a defined contribution scheme, then the end benefits are not exactly known and are dependent on funding requirements – again actuarially determined. An occupational defined contribution scheme, such as a money purchase group scheme is one such scheme. Group and individual personal pension schemes are others. There is a great variety of these – personal pension plans (PPPs), self-invested personal pensions (SIPPs) for the self employed;

SSAS – small self-administered schemes; Executive Personal Pension schemes (EPPs) are examples of occupational schemes.

A combination of pension funds plus an investment and savings portfolio, as well as property investments and other diversified investments would form the basis for a retirement plan.

There is no question that for most people, pension funding will form the bulk of their retirement planning portfolios. Proper structuring and asset allocation using available disposable income needs to be done, taking into account risk assessment and the types of investments best suited to your risk profile.

Your age is important, as is the number of years of work or employment left to accumulate wealth and then to manage it effectively. Protecting your assets and wealth is equally important. If you become disabled or die, or if a spouse does, then your plans need to be protected. It makes common sense to protect pension payments, and to limit the risks associated with wealth loss.

You may do a tremendous job in building up your retirement portfolio, but at retirement, making decisions can be crucial. The right decisions can significantly increase your income, improve your wealth and protect your position; the wrong ones can mean less income, or wasting wealth.

Retirement Countdown Planning should begin at least 10 years before retirement date. It becomes more urgent as the retirement date looms, and different actions are required at the various stages. For example, a 55-year old retiring at age 60 would like to see more pension funding and possibly a scaling down of other less important employee benefits. Up to two years from retirement, you would want to be eliminating debt, making sure the mortgage is paid off and buying new white goods for your house.

With the heralding of stakeholder pensions, the pensions environment is changing. For the first time, children can begin pension plans (or have it begun for the child by a parent or grandparent), and those without relevant earnings can also have a pension scheme. Tax reliefs on contributions immediately increase the return of the investment.

Retirement planning is not only about building investments and pension plans for your old age. It is also about setting objectives, and doing other things, such as tax planning, estate planning, planning with tax-free lump sums, working closely with employers and the best use of employee benefits for wealth creation.

Pensions Simplified is an essential part of the retirement planning mix.

2

Different Types of Pension Fund

Broadly speaking, there are two main differences in pension funds. Every other variation springs from these two types. Pension funds can be divided into either defined benefit pension schemes or defined contribution pension schemes.

Defined Benefit Pension Scheme

This type of scheme is best typified by what is known as the **final salary scheme**. *Defined* benefit because the recipient knows exactly how much his or her pension fund will be, based on a pre-determined formula. The unknown fact is how much funding is required to make the defined benefit a reality. This is an actuarial calculation based on factors such as age, length of time to go to retirement, the amount of money currently in the fund, interest rates and investment returns as well as other factors.

Nowadays, very few new final salary schemes are being taken out by businesses. The reasons are numerous, but in the main, the very high cost of funding required by the employer to maintain final salary scheme benefits, and the new accounting provision for defined benefit schemes in the balance sheets of companies (where, if the scheme is under-funded, it can reduce profits of the company).

However, most large companies have a final salary scheme for their employees, as does the Government for its employees, and this type of scheme is undoubtedly one of the best forms of pension provision. A recent trend is to move from a defined benefit scheme to a defined contribution scheme, and many employers have taken this route to reduce future pension funding costs.

The defined benefit pension scheme allows both employer and employee to contribute to it. The employee can contribute an extra amount to boost eventual retirement benefits through what is known as the AVC, or additional voluntary contribution scheme. The AVC is with the main scheme provider to the employer. Alternatively, the employee can contribute to a product provider of his or her choice – this is known as a free-standing AVC. In recent times, the stakeholder pension contract is being used more for AVC type contributions, as a cheaper alternative.

Normal retirement age

If the scheme was approved before the 25th July 1991, then retirement ages usually fall between the ages of 60 and 70 for men and 55 and 70 for women. However, if a woman is at least a 20% director, then the retirement age minimum is age 60. For schemes set up after the 25th July 1991 the age range is 60 to 75 for all members.

You can retire early (from age 50), but with reduced pension benefits, or later than the retirement age of the fund with increased benefits, but subject to a maximum of 2/3 of final remuneration. If not a 20% director and you have over 40 years service, you may qualify for a pension of up to 75% of final remuneration on actual retirement after the normal retirement date.

Defined Contribution Pension Scheme

This type of pension scheme is based on a *pre-determined level of contributions* to make up the pension fund or pension scheme (as opposed to a defined benefit pension scheme, where the contribution levels are largely unknown from year to year, and actuarially determined). Contributions may be set for employer-sponsored defined contribution schemes where, for example, the employer pays 6% of salary and the employee pays 3%; or may vary, for example, if an individual is self-employed and makes contributions based on the

Inland Revenue limits each year.

At the end of the day, you get what you pay for under a defined contribution scheme. The value of the pension scheme itself depends on the contributions made and how well they are invested, the costs of the scheme, and other factors.

At retirement, the value of the pension fund can be apportioned for tax-free cash and a reduced pension, or no tax-free cash and a higher pension. The way in which pensions are paid also differs from a defined benefit scheme. A defined contribution scheme pays a pension through purchasing an annuity for the individual at retirement date. A defined benefit scheme, like a final salary scheme, may also use annuities to buy the pension, but are not restricted to this route – pensions could be paid from the fund itself, from the sale of assets, or even out of employer's cash flow.

There are different types of defined contribution pension schemes available, each type having its own set of rules and limitations. Most schemes are approved by the Inland Revenue, but some may be unapproved (like a FURBS).

The most common types of defined contribution pension schemes are given below, as well as their uses.

Personal Pension Plan Scheme (PPP)

Largely used by the self-employed. Employees without employer pension schemes may contribute (or the employer may do so) to a personal pension plan. Must have net relevant earnings to qualify, and contributions are based on age and taxable income. Minimum age 18. Can retire between age 50 and 75.

Self-invested Personal Pension Plan (SIPP)

A personal pension plan where the individual decides how and where the contributions are to be invested. They are cheap to set up. However, most SIPP providers expect large annual contributions. A wide range of investment possibilities includes investing in residential and commercial properties (not your own, though), traded endowment policies and other choices. Contributions are as for the personal pension regime, and retirement ages.

Stakeholder Pension Plan (SPP)

Based on a Personal Pension Plan, but with a lower cost charging structure, and other benefits such as cat-marked standards. Used by the self-employed, employees where there is no employer pension fund availability, employees who are on an employer's pension fund, but earning less than £30,000 per annum. Minimum age, at birth. Retirement age, from 50 to 75.

You do not require taxable earnings, and can contribute up to £3,600 a year. Anyone can have a stakeholder pension plan, including children. The contribution is made net of basic rate tax (£2,808).

Group Personal Pension Plans (GPPP)

A Group Personal pension Plan is one where an employer sets up a number of PPPs for employers within a group arrangement to achieve economies of scale and cheaper pension administration costs. Each individual employee has a personal pension plan account within the group arrangement. Usually the employer contributes as well as the employee. If employer contributions are 3% or more, then this satisfies the stakeholder pension equivalent for employers. There can be flexibility within the grouping for individual retirement arrangements. A GPPP can be used to contract out of SERPS, when the scheme is known as an appropriate personal pension scheme (APPS).

The maximum age to contribute to is 74, but retirement age 75. Premiums paid can achieve tax relief at your highest marginal rate of tax as an employee, whilst the employer making contributions has them allowed against corporation tax. NI contributions can also be avoided through making contributions. The fund grows free of all taxes and part of the fund can be taken tax free at retirement. Widows and widowers qualify for pension benefits, and on death, benefits under trust avoid tax. GPPPs fall under the personal pension scheme rules, not the rules of an occupational pension fund. They also allow employers to avoid most of the requirements of the Pensions Act 1995.

The new 'defined contribution regime' is an attempt by the Government to merge the stakeholder and personal pension regimes. From October 2001, employers with more than 4 employees must offer access to a designated stakeholder pension scheme. Employers are exempt if a GPPP is offered, but only if it makes a contribution of at least 3% of basic pay, and other conditions.

Retirement Annuity (RA)
Although not offered since 1988, individuals may have existing RA plans. If so, they can still contribute to these plans, and make carry forward and carry back pension contributions (personal pension plans lost the ability to carry forward contributions after April 2001). Contributions are based on net relevant earnings and a formula of age and earnings. Retirement ages are from 60-75. Mainly for the self-employed.

Executive Pension Plan (EPP)
This is an occupational pension scheme for an executive, or a spouse, for example, employed in the business. An EPP has an accelerated funding programme depending on the member's age, sex and years to retirement. Retirement dates are between ages 50 and 75.

Small Self-Administered Pension Scheme (SSAS)
An occupational pension scheme which has fewer than 12 members. With the same retirement range as EPPs of 50-75, the SSAS is mainly for company controlling directors, partners, or selected senior employees. Special rules restrict contribution levels by directors, as well as the types of investments undertaken. However, the SSAS can invest in commercial property, take out mortgages, buy shares in a private company (as well as the sponsoring company). Pension benefits are calculated as for occupational pension schemes.

Money Purchase pension schemes (MP)
MPs are occupational pension schemes, with defined contributions.

Defined Contribution schemes (DC)
The new defined contribution regime for pensions has merged personal pensions and stakeholder pensions together with money purchase occupational pension funds that opt in.

All of the above types of pension scheme depend on contributions being made and invested to provide a pension and tax-free cash. The amount of tax-free cash and pensions or annuities payable depends on the type of pension fund arrangement. Occupational pension schemes have different rules and formulae to schemes for the self-employed, for example.

Additional Voluntary Contributions (AVC)
An AVC pension scheme is where additional voluntary contributions are paid to an occupational pension scheme in addition to normal contributions, to obtain extra pension benefits. Funds saved in this way boost the retirement pension from the main scheme. Up to 15% of salary (including the value of taxable benefits, such as a company car,) may be contributed to an AVC scheme.

Free-Standing AVCs (FSAVC)
Employees may make additional voluntary contributions into a money purchase fund of their choice, within Inland Revenue limits. This means they can make their contributions to a product provider that does not provide the main pension scheme benefits.

FURBS
A FURBS is a Funded Unapproved Retirement Benefit Scheme, used either as a top-up to other pension schemes, and usually when the other pension scheme is at the pensions cap and can accept no further contributions, or where there is no other pension scheme and the employee requires a fund consisting of a tax-free lump sum cash payment, rather than a pension which is taxable. The contributions made are tax deductible to the employer, but taxable in the hands of the employee and national insurance contributions are payable. The fund itself is taxed at rates below the maximum personal income tax rate, and the proceeds are tax free. There are wide investment powers for a FURBS, making it attractive to high rated taxpayers as well as others seeking a separate home for their retirement funding.

19

Other Pension Schemes

Other pension schemes would include those used to transfer pensions from one scheme to another. For example, a Section 32 Buyout Bond can receive pension transfers. There is also the Individual Pension Account (IPA), which introduces the concept of a pooled pensions investment for savings. The idea is to give one control over a pension savings vehicle, investing in gilts, collective investments and quoted shares, and is similar to the American 401k pensions savings plan.

3

Pensions for the Self-employed and Those Who are not Members of the Employer's Pension Scheme

The **self-employed** are those working as sole traders, or essentially 'one man band' small companies, treated by the Inland Revenue as being self-employed. If self-employed, you could be working for yourself, or have employees working in your business. The general rule is that the self-employed are governed by the personal pension rules and may make pension contributions based on their 'net relevant earnings' to a personal pension plan (or to a retirement annuity account – although these were discontinued after 1988).

Those not members of the employer's pension scheme can also contribute to a personal pension plan on the same basis as that outlined below for the self-employed.

The self-employed can also contribute to a stakeholder pension plan, especially in poor business years where they may not have sufficient income, and therefore no relevant earnings for normal pension contributions. Stakeholder pensions will take gross contributions of up to £3,600 (£2,808 net) without the need for net relevant earnings.

Contributions to Inland Revenue approved pension schemes are tax allowable against taxable income, and contributions made reduce taxable income, and thereby tax payable.

The pension fund grows tax free and at retirement date (between age 50 and 75), can provide a tax-free lump sum and a reduced pension (annuity), or a higher pension without a tax-free lump sum.

The choice is yours. Usually though, most people take the tax-free lump sum as they feel they can control their own investments better, and may have uses for it beyond making investments, such as reducing mortgages or paying off debt.

If you have an existing retirement annuity fund, then continue with payments to this, as tax-free lump sums may be higher. You can still do carry-back carry-forward contributions (which have ended for those on personal pension schemes) to relieve previous unutilised tax reliefs from the past 6-7 years, and they are not subject to the pensions earning cap. However, the contribution levels are lower than those for a personal pension plan; the normal retirement age is 60 (not 50 as with a personal pensions plan); employers cannot make contributions to a retirement annuity (they can with a personal pension plan); and income draw-down is not possible through a retirement annuity (a transfer must first be made to a personal pension plan).

Older retirement annuity policies will only allow a refund of premiums plus, say, 4-5% on death, although the life office can change this to a return of fund, if the right approaches are made.

The following are the maximum contribution levels to a personal pension plan and to a retirement annuity, as a percentage of earnings. Stakeholder pensions contributions are not subject to earnings.

Age on the first day of the tax year	Stakeholder	Personal Pension %*		Retirement Annuity %*	
Any age	£3,600 p.a. gross £2,808 net	Max Contribution**	£	Max Contribution	
35 or less		17.5	17,010	17.5	no max
36-45		20.0	19,440	17.5	
46-50		25.0	24,300	17.5	
51-55		30.0	29,160	20.0	
56-60		35.0	34,030	22.5	
61 or more		40.0	38,880	27.5	

* Net relevant earnings are usually taxable earnings after deductions of

allowable expenses. It can include the taxable value of benefits, e.g. company car.
** The pensions cap in 2002/03 tax year is £97,200. Maximum contributions are based on the percentage applied against the pensions earnings cap. It does not apply to retirement annuity contributions.

If Smith has net relevant earnings of £50,000, and he is age 52, then he could contribute 30% x £50,000 = £15,000 to a personal pension plan and £10,000 (20% x £50,000) to a retirement annuity, if he has one.

If Jones was age 52 and she had net relevant earnings of £150,000, she could contribute 30% x £120,000 = £45,000 capped at £29,160 to a personal pension plan, but could contribute £30,000 to a retirement annuity, which is not capped, for the same earnings, if she has one.

The type of pension plans that the self-employed can enjoy include regular premium contribution plans, for example £100 per month; or a single premium contribution of say £5,000 a year, or whenever. Single premiums are cheaper than regular premiums, as their costs are less. You can also have a Self-Invested Personal Pension Plan (SIPP), where you direct how the plan is to be invested. You have very wide investment options, from property to even investing into other pension fund investments. A SIPP's investment funds can be spread over a number of investment houses, and is more flexible at retirement, with regard to options.

The Inland Revenue can help you to save by giving generous tax reliefs to you. Contributions are now paid net, putting pension contributions on a similar basis to the employed. All contributions are made net at 22%, the basic rate taxpayer's rate (even if only a 10% taxpayer). The Inland Revenue pays the difference to your pension fund. If a higher rate taxpayer, you claim the difference through your tax return or PAYE coding.

For example, if you are a 40% taxpayer, and wish to contribute £5,000 this year, you only pay (£5,000 – £1,100 (22%) = £3,900 and the Inland Revenue pays the rest into your fund to make up the £5,000. You then also claim (40-22% = 18% = £900) back through your tax return.

Your fund then grows tax free and at retirement, 25% can come out tax free. You could have had a total of 65% worth of tax reliefs through investing in pensions. It's probably one of the only times you will thank the Inland Revenue!

Getting your life assurance tax deductible

Up to 5th April 2001, 5% of your net relevant earnings could be used to purchase term life assurance to provide lump sum benefits for dependants, tax free, in trust, which also avoids inheritance tax. The premiums attract full income tax relief at your highest rates. The policy is a term policy for death before age 75.

From 6th April 2001, the 5% of net relevant earnings reduces to 10% of the contributions payable, which may be used to purchase term assurance. This includes employer's contributions. These assurance premiums are deductible from taxable earnings, and form part of the pension contribution payable. However, it will now no longer be possible to have a pension policy with no contributions and only life assurance premiums, as the tax deductible life assurance premiums are based on the pension contributions made.

Examples

	Pre 5th April 2001			Post 6th April 2001
Net relevant earnings	Contribution %		5% NRE	10% of Contributions
(i) £20,000 at age 35	17.5% -5%: 12.5%	+	£1,000	17.5%: 10% x £3,500 = £350 term ass
Contribution mix	£3,500: £2,500	+	£1,000	3,500: – £350 (term ass.) = £3,150
				pension contribution

- On the old basis, contribute £2,500 or nothing to pension fund and £1,000 buys term assurance death benefits.
- On the new basis, contribute £3,150 to pension fund and £350 buys term assurance
- Both tax deductible at the full level of 17.5% of net relevant earnings for a person age 35 and below.

	Pre 5th April 2001			Post 6th April 2001
Net relevant earnings	Contribution %		5% NRE	10% of Contributions
(2) £50,000 at age 51	30%- 5% : 25%	+	£2,500	30%: 10% x £15,000 + £1,500 term ass
Contribution mix	£15,000 : £12,500	+	£2,500	£15,000: – £1,500 (term ass.) =
				£13,500 pension contribution

- On the old basis, contribute £12,500 or nothing to the pension fund and £2,500 buys term assurance death benefits.
- On the new basis, contribute £13,500 to pension fund and £1,500 buys term assurance
- Both tax deductible at the full level of 30% of net relevant earnings for a person age 51 in this case.

The self-employed can make tax efficient pension contributions and also contribute to life assurance term policies, that have tax deductible premiums in the contribution mix. However, the new position after 6th April 2001 means that less is available to pay for tax deductible life assurance than before.

4

Occupational Pension Schemes – if in Work

An occupational pension schemes is another name for an employer sponsored pension scheme. Occupational pension schemes will fall into three main categories:

(1) Defined Benefit Schemes (DBS)
(2) Defined Contribution Schemes (DCS) and
(3) AVCs and FSAVCs. Stakeholder pension schemes may now substitute for FSAVCs as a better deal.

We also have a 'defined contribution regime', not to be confused with an occupational pension scheme with defined contributions.

1. Defined benefit schemes

A defined benefit pension scheme is best described as an Inland Revenue approved and exempt pension scheme, designed to pay out a defined benefit at retirement date, or earlier or later than the normal retirement date. These are usually final salary or average final salary pension schemes, based on final remuneration and years of service.

A move from one employer to another may mean a lower pension benefit, even if both offer a final salary pension scheme. If the former employer had a final salary defined benefit pension scheme, you may have to make that previous pension scheme 'paid up' and not transfer the benefit, as a pension would be based on your years' service in that pension scheme together with the years of service in your employer's new final salary pension scheme at your usual retirement age. However, if the new employer's pension scheme is different from the former employer's pension scheme, for example, you are moving from a defined contribution scheme (money purchase) to a defined benefit scheme (final salary), then it may be to your advantage to pay into your new employer's defined benefit scheme to buy what is called 'back service'.

That is if the rules allow it to be done.

As the defined benefit pension scheme is based on years' service, the less the years' service, the less the end pension benefit will be. An actuarial calculation may say that you can buy back 5 years of service for £50,000. You have £50,000 in your previous employer's pension fund, and make the transfer. You then work for your new employer for, say, 15 years, but the back-service purchased gives you 20 years service with the new employer for the pensions formula.

Most things can be negotiated and employees coming and going from one employment to another should not be afraid to negotiate a better position for themselves.

With a defined benefit pension scheme, at the retirement date of the employee, a pension will be payable based on a formula of years ('N') served with the employer over a pre-determined factor (usually 60ths) times final salary ('FS' -sometimes based on a formula for the final salary or average salary, usually the best three years in the last five or seven years).

This will be limited to 2/3 of the earnings cap, currently £97,200 in 2002/03.

The above is the formula to be used with at least 20 years service. With less than 20 years service, the maximum pension is scaled down by 1/30th for each year less.

If you joined an employer's scheme before 17th March 1987, then a different maximum accrual rate can apply. This means you could get a maximum 2/3 pension after only ten years (instead of 20 years) service.

Example

Jenny has worked for Excellent Fashions PLC for 25 years before retiring at age 60. She joined the pension scheme on the 1st June 1970. Her pension scheme is a final salary defined benefits scheme. The factor is 60ths. The final salary is based on an average of the best three years out of the last seven years, which in her case are the last three years, averaging £32,000 as a final salary.

Her pension will be: 25 years/60ths x £32,000 per annum, (limited to 2/3 of £97,200, the pensions earnings cap, which is a limit of £64,800.)

25/60 x £32,000 = £13,333 gross pension per year. The pension received is taxable at source at basic rate and Jenny will receive a net pension after tax.

Jenny is also entitled to a tax-free lump sum. The lump sum paid is actually paid from giving up some pension benefits. This is called a commutation.

The maximum tax-free lump sum payable to Jenny depends on when she became a member of the pension scheme, the rules of the particular scheme and her length of service to retirement.

The formula for a tax-free lump sum is based on the greater of 3/80ths of final remuneration for each year of service (up to a maximum of 40 years) or 2.25 times the amount of the member's pension before commutation, whichever is the greater.

This is in turn limited to a maximum tax-free lump sum of the lesser of 1.5 times final remuneration or 1.5 times the pensions earning cap, currently 1.5 x £97,200 = £145,800 for 2002/03).

The formula for tax-free lump sums depends on when Jenny joined her employer's pension fund. If she had joined before 1st June 1989 but on or after 17th March 1987, then the maximum tax-free lump sum would be the lesser of £150,000 or 1.5 times remuneration, so long as she had clocked up at least 20 years of service and with a pension of 2/3 of final remuneration.

If she joined the pension scheme before 17th March 1987, then the maximum tax-free lump sum is 1.5 times her final remuneration without any upper limit. However, she must have at least 20 years service at retirement to do so. Lesser service would have a different accrual rate, as it would if Jenny retired early.

In Jenny's case, as she joined the scheme on the 1st June 1970, she would be entitled to the greater of 3/80ths of final remuneration for each year of service or 2.25 times the amount of her pension before commutation, whichever is the greater, so:

	3/80 x 25 years x £32,000	= £30,000
or		
	2.25 x £13,333	= £29,999

Maximum test:

	lesser of 1.5 x £32,000	= £48,000
or		
	1.5 x £97,200	= £145,800 (1.5. times the earnings cap)

The result is that Jenny can take £30,000 tax-free cash, which is well within the maximum tax-free cash allowable to her under the rules. In addition she would have a pension of £13,333 per annum gross, which is taxable.

2. Defined contributions occupational pension schemes

Under these types of pension scheme, the employer determines how much to spend on pension contributions. It is then able to budget for pensions scheme contributions and not incur pension funding liabilities by not being able to adequately fund a pension scheme. Previously called 'money purchase pension schemes'.

The type of funding could be as a percentage of employees' pay or even a set fixed figure per employee. Employees can also contribute. You may have a situation, where a scheme is contributory, and the employer pays say 10% of salary and the employee 5%; or non-contributory, where the employer pays 10% and the employee nothing. The percentages differ, depending on what can be afforded and agreed between the parties.

The money contributed is invested either through a life office, or fund manager or stockbroker to provide a fund for each employee at the retirement date. Each employee will therefore have a retirement 'pot' containing the company contributions share and his or her own contribution share with any growth in the underlying funds being added.

The pension pot provided for each employee, may, at retirement date, be taken as a pension or as a reduced pension and a tax-free lump sum. Alternatively, the tax-free lump sum may be taken and the balance of the fund placed in an income draw-down fund before a pension or annuity is taken by age 75.

Inland Revenue and pension legislation applies with regard to funding limits, the pensions earnings cap (£97,200 in 2002/03), final salary definitions and length of service requirements.

These Inland Revenue limits apply irrespective of whether the scheme is a defined benefits or a defined contribution scheme. With a *final salary based defined benefits scheme*, the risk of providing a pension and tax-free cash according to the formula, lies with the employer; with a *defined contribution scheme*, the risk of investment performance and adequate contributions having been made, lies with the employee. The size of the ultimate pension depends on the size of the pension fund, investment performance and quantum of contributions.

Employers can claim their contributions as a corporation tax expense, whilst employees can claim up to 15% of their taxable remuneration (including the value of taxable benefits, such as the company car value).

Exempt occupational pension schemes do not pay income, corporation or capital gains tax on fund investments. Pension funds cannot reclaim tax credits on dividends from UK companies, which will reduce overall investment returns in any pension fund. This may require schemes to make additional funding to meet pension fund value targets.

At retirement, a taxable pension is paid from the pension fund, usually funded through the internal purchase of an annuity. In addition, a tax-free lump sum is payable, usually at up to 1.5 times final salary, and various rules apply as to maximum amounts (see the section on tax-free lump sums).

In the 2002/03 tax year, the maximum pension at normal retirement date is limited to £64,800 (2/3 of the pensions earnings cap) after 20 years service, and the maximum tax-free cash is £145,800. This is because the pensions cap acts as a brake on benefits. If a member dies before his or her spouse and this is after retirement, then a spouse's pension of up to 2/3 of the member's pension may be payable.

The example given for the defined benefits scheme above, uses the same occupational pension scheme rules for pensions and tax-free lump sums, as well as Inland Revenue limits.

The defined contribution regime

The defined contribution regime includes defined contribution occupational schemes, stakeholder pension schemes and personal pension schemes.

From 6th April 2001, members of a defined benefit scheme can contribute to a defined contribution regime scheme where:

(i) earnings for any of the previous five tax years have not exceeded £30,000 (but not taking into account tax years before 2000/01)

(ii) the individual concerned has not been a controlling director during the current or five preceding tax years

What this means is that you can contribute a maximum additional amount because of the stakeholder pension rules of £3,600, in addition to the 15% of earnings to a defined benefit scheme. The maximum limit under the earnings cap for the 15% is £14,580. These additional benefits are ignored when calculating the overall maximum benefits from the defined benefit scheme, but AVC benefits are included in the calculation.

31

3. AVC/FSAVC

Additional Voluntary Contributions (AVC) are paid in addition to normal contributions, to secure extra benefits. The AVC is offered by the same pension provider to the main pension scheme and is administered by the employer. The free-standing AVC (FSAVC) can be purchased from any product provider and gives more investment control to the individual. The AVC cannot be taken as a lump sum in cash (unless pre 1987), but can increase the value of your overall fund and give you additional pension benefits and increase the level of tax-free cash through the main pension fund.

Contributions are tax deductible up to 15% of your remuneration. The 15% includes contributions required by the scheme, and for contracted-out money purchase schemes, employee rebates. Remuneration also includes the value of benefits in kind. The maximum contribution is limited by the pensions earning cap and in 2002/03 the cap is 15% x £97,200 = £14,580. This means a maximum of £1,215.00 can be saved per month if salary or remuneration was at the level of the cap.

Contributions are paid net of basic rate tax, thus saving cash flow.

With the advent of the stakeholder pension regime and the grouping together of various defined contribution pension plans under one umbrella, employees may make contributions into AVCs, FSAVCs at 15% of remuneration as defined, as well as £3,600 gross (£2,808) net in a stakeholder pension scheme. As most employees do not have sufficient cash available to invest into both stakeholder pension plans and an FSAVC, and because stakeholder offers far more flexible options, including tax-free cash, the trend is for those employees earning under £30,000 to contribute to a stakeholder plan rather than to FSAVCs. However, if they can afford it, they can contribute to both, and stakeholder benefits will not be aggregated with occupational scheme benefits when maximum benefits tests are being done.

5

Stakeholder Pensions

Description

The Stakeholder pension scheme was introduced through the Welfare Reform and Pensions Act 1999. It is the plain vanilla version of a personal pension plan, and designed to enable a pension to be possible for all. In fact, for the first time, the concept of having to have 'net relevant earnings' to contribute to a pension scheme is swept away, and non-earning spouses and children can now have a pension scheme.

Premium contributions

The stakeholder pension scheme is designed to give pension benefits to those retiring between ages 50 and 75. Premiums can be regular (with a minimum of £20) or single premiums and in both cases cannot exceed £3,600 per annum without reference to earnings. There is no frequency of premium payment, so long as the minimum of £20 is made each time.

Where there is reference to earnings, then contributions in excess of the £3,600 will be allowed in accordance with current personal pension scheme age limits, which are:

Ages between	% Contribution
Any Age	£3,600 and no earnings required
Under 36	17.5% of net relevant earnings
36-45	20%
46-50	25%
51-55	30%
56-60	35%
61-74	40%

If a member of an occupational pension scheme

If you are an employee with an occupational pension scheme, then five years previous earnings can be taken into account – to not have exceeded £30,000 in any one year – however tax years before 2000/01 are not taken into account.

Members of a defined benefit scheme can contribute £3,600 to a stakeholder pension scheme, in addition to 15% of taxable earnings that can be paid to a defined benefit scheme. For example, an employee earning say £25,000 (under £30,000) can be a member of an occupational pension scheme, contribute £3,600 (net £2,808) to a stakeholder pension scheme, and 15% of taxable earnings to an AVC or FSAVC scheme.

It should be borne in mind that stakeholder costs will be lower than most other schemes. To this extent, most will prefer the stakeholder pension route, rather than the FSAVC/AVC route for both the £3,600 and the 15% of taxable earnings. Stakeholder is generally being used in preference to the FSAVC pension as being more flexible and cheaper.

At retirement, the benefits from the stakeholder pensions are not taken into account when calculating the overall maximum benefits from the occupational pension defined benefits scheme, whereas AVC/FSAVC contributions would be so included.

What if you stop work?

If an individual is contributing over £3,600 per year and stops work, then he or she can contribute that higher amount for a further 5 years. After that period is up, then the contribution limit reverts to the £3,600 per year level.

Effectively, contributions could be based on earnings going back 10 years. Where relevant earnings are used to justify contributions above the £3,600 per year, then you can use earnings in any of the previous 5 years if they were higher than earnings in the current year. Thus, if your best year for earnings was 5 years ago and you made contributions at that level for 5 years, then you could have made contributions based on an earnings figure from 10 years previously.

Who can take out a stakeholder pension?

You can take out the pension scheme yourself, or take one out for someone else, such as a child or grandchild. Alternatively, an employer can set up or designate a scheme (in fact, legally all employers with 4 or more employees must designate a stakeholder pension scheme or face large fines).

It is most suitable for self-employed individuals, or those employees who are not in an occupational pension scheme. If you are an employee in an occupational pensions scheme, earning under £30,000 p.a. you qualify for stakeholder (in addition to your occupational scheme membership). However, you must not have been a controlling director during the current or any one of the five previous tax years.

Pensions flexibility means you can provide dependants with a pension scheme. Even a baby can have a pension scheme, and need never make a pension contribution ever again – you as parent or grandparent can build up a tax efficient fund for a child.

For example, minors can invest £3,600 a year each into a stakeholder pension without the need for earnings. As pension contributions are made net of basic rate tax of 22%, you need only invest £2,808 to have an actual investment of £3,600.

Tax relief on contributions

All contributions are paid into your stakeholder pension plan net of basic rate tax. This applies to those with no income, as well as the self-employed.

If you wish to contribute £100 per month, then you only actually pay £88 and the Inland Revenue pays £22. Basic rate of tax is 22% in 2002/03.

You can carry back a pension contribution to a previous tax year (or if no relevant earnings in that year, to the year previous to that one) and obtain tax relief in that year for the contribution. The payment must be made by the 31st January in the year following the tax year to which the payment is being carried back. You must also elect to do this before or at the same time as the payment.

Carry forward of unused pensions relief was abolished from 6th April 2001.

Contracting out of SERPS/State Second Pension

Age related rebates to stakeholder schemes are possible for those contracting out and for any stakeholder scheme, the rebate is based on the stakeholder's actual salary in excess of the lower earnings limit (even though the state second pension will be based on £9,500. You can only contract out if employed and earning a salary).

Life cover

10% of stakeholder pensions contributions qualify for life cover. Essentially, this is a way to get part or all of your life cover premiums tax deductible. The older you are, the less the amount of cover that can be provided in this way.

Life cover can only be term cover up to the maximum retirement age. No whole of life cover is allowable.

Term cover provided under stakeholder is 10% of the contributions made. Under the personal pensions regime, it was 5% of net relevant earnings, which could be higher than 10% of contributions.

Stakeholder cannot have a waiver of premium benefit incorporated into it. Waiver of premium can be a stand-alone policy though and is always advisable if you can get it. What it does is protect you if you become disabled and cannot work nor pay premiums as a result. The pension contributions are paid for you. This separate contract is not tax deductible (whereas waiver of premium usually is), but the premiums are usually very small, and tax relief is negligible.

The pension fund itself

The contributions are made to the pension fund. They are paid net of basic rate tax, even for non-earners. Once in the pension fund, these contributions are invested into the selected investment accounts where the growth is tax free.

The widely publicised minimum standards for stakeholder pensions means that the maximum charge will be 1% of the fund value per annum. No other charges from the fund will be allowed.

There may well be other charges – for advice or other services – but these have to be paid for separately, not from the fund.

Most types of investment options are available, including with profits.

At retirement

Retirement can be between the ages of 50 and 75. At retirement, you have a choice of either taking 25% in cash tax free from the fund with a reduced annuity (or pension), or taking a full pension, with no tax-free cash. The pension or annuity taken is taxable. Much will depend on your circumstances at retirement, as to which option is taken up.

The retirement date can be flexible and you do not need to actually retire to receive your benefits.

Death before retirement

If you die before retirement, then death benefits could be a return of fund plus interest, and any amount insured for under the contract.

Employer's responsibilities

Employers with 5 or less employees are exempt from providing stakeholder access. They are also exempt if there is an occupational pension scheme, so long as employees can join within 12 months of starting work. Those under 18 or within 5 years of retirement can also be excluded.

Another employer exemption is where the employer has a Group Personal Pension Scheme (GPP), contributes at least 3% of basic pay, has no exit penalties, and is available within 3 months of joining the employer (except if under age 18).

Other exemptions also apply. For example, where employees earn below the lower earnings limit, stakeholder does not have to be offered to them. One would think this is the very group that stakeholder pensions should be directed at, but the Government obviously feels they cannot afford even the most basic pension contribution.

If the employer is not exempt, then it must offer access to a stakeholder scheme within 3 months of joining the employer.

The employer need only designate a scheme (choose a prospective supplier), not operate a scheme, or recommend one. The employer then consults with employees as to the proposed designated scheme, giving them necessary information; operates a payroll system to deduct contributions from pay; and maintains stakeholder compliance.

6

State Pension Scheme

Firstly, there is no actuarially funded state pension scheme, like an employers' pension scheme. Those in work pay in national insurance contributions at a predetermined amount, those on state pensions receive their share as the state pension weekly or monthly.

The state provides pension funds in two distinct parts. The first part is the 'old age pension' or the basic state scheme; the second part is known as SERPS, the State Earnings Related Pension Scheme. SERPS is gradually being replaced by the State Second Pension (S2P).

The State pension age was 65 for men and 60 for women. It will be equalised upwards for women to age 65 from April 2010. Women will have to work an extra 5 years before the state pension benefits them in the future.

The new pension age of 65 for all will affect women born after April 1955. Women born after April 1950 and before April 1955 will have a state pension age of between 60 and 65. Women born before April 1950 will have a state pension age of 60.

What is it worth?

The basic old age state pension for a single person in 2002/03 is £75.50 per week for a single person and £120.70 per week for a married couple.

The state basic pension has been rising each year by the RPI as at September in each year and applied from April of the following year.

Increases in the state basic pension after retirement are linked to the RPI – the retail prices index – and not the AEI, the average earnings index, which rises at a higher rate. Benefits are therefore worth less than if they were linked to the AEI. from April 2003, there will be an extra £100 for single pensioners, and £160 for pensioner couples, with a minimum guaranteed 2.5% p.a. from 2004.

Can you take early retirement?

You can, but don't expect anything from the state until the designated day arrives at 65 for men and 60 for women currently.

However, you can postpone your state retirement benefits from retirement age onwards for a slightly higher benefit for each year deferred.

Can you take a lump sum?

No lump sum rights can be accrued. There is no tax-free lump sum, nor can the state scheme be commuted for a lump sum, nor is there a death in service lump sum. However, there are very small bereavement allowances, should you die in the tax year. Every little bit helps, but don't get too excited.

How do you qualify?

For a man, he must have paid sufficient national insurance contributions. For a woman, she may claim on the record of her own or her spouse's contributions. Whichever route produces the best result is acceptable.

The maximum pension is achieved by making contributions during 90% of your working life between ages 16 to 65. If not at that level, then voluntary contributions can be made to get there. However, these voluntary contributions are not tax deductible.

Who to contact

Apply to the Department for Work & Pensions, formerly the DSS for form BR19 to establish what your pension benefits are.

7

SERPS

The State Earnings Related Pension Scheme (SERPS) is the additional component to the basic state pension scheme.

SERPS is not available to the self-employed, only to those in employment. The Government is desperate to get out of long-term pension provision, and SERPS is being phased out, to be replaced with the State Second Pension.

For years, the Government has been encouraging people to contract out of SERPS, and to make their own provision, using the rebates from the national insurance contributions to do so. It may or may not mean that you are better off if you do decide to contract out of SERPS, but there is always an opportunity to contract back in if this helps you.

How much does SERPS pay?

Up to April 1999, the SERPS pension amounted to 25% of the average pensionable earnings of the best 20 years before retirement, increased by the AEI (average earnings index).

From April 2000, the 25% figure above reduced to 20% of average revalued lifetime earnings (as opposed to average pensionable earnings), and will be phased in from April 2000 to April 2010 for earnings after 6 April 1988.

Pensionable earnings fall between the lower earnings limit (LEL) of £72 per week and the upper earnings limit of £575 per week, and are known as band earnings. The annual rise will be reflected by the RPI not the AEI, meaning the value of the benefit will be even less.

Contracting out of SERPS

If you think private enterprise can beat the state scheme, then contracting out of the SERPS could be an option.

What this means is that an age-related rebate is paid into an occupational pension scheme or a wide range of employee sponsored schemes.

Final salary scheme	Must provide a pension at least equivalent to SERPS. This is the GMP, or Guaranteed Minimum Pension. Annually it must increase by the RPI or at least 3%. After April 1997, a GMP is no longer payable, and increases of 5% or the RPI if lower, and no top up payments from the state scheme are available.
Group Money Purchase and Appropriate Personal Pension schemes (APPS)	Do not have to provide a GMP when contracting out. Must provide protected rights benefits instead, which will purchase an annuity paying a 3% escalation annually. GMP and protected rights only paid from state pension age.
Personal pension schemes (PPP), Free standing AVC schemes	Contracted out PPPs receive the rebate at the end of the tax year in one lump sum. Employees can contract out individually through an APPS - appropriate personal pension scheme, or an FSAVC.They continue with contracted- in NI contributions, as does the employer.

The national insurance rebates are age related. These range from 4% of middle band earnings for the youngest ages, to 9% for the oldest – from age 47 age attained on 5th April 1997.

COMPS – contracted out money purchase schemes pay a percentage of middle band earnings into the scheme ranging from 2.4% for the youngest to 8.4% for the oldest.

43

$\overline{\underline{8}}$

State 2nd Pension (S2P)

SERPS will be phased out and replaced by the new State Second Pension (S2P), meaning that lower earners (£3,432 – £18,500) will be better off.

The state second pension will gradually replace SERPS, beginning in April 2002 as an earnings related scheme, and later with a benefit payable at a flat rate.

It will be possible to contract out of S2P in the following way:

- Enhanced rebate benefit under personal pension schemes

- For a stakeholder pension the rebate is based on the stakeholder's actual salary in excess of the lower earnings limit, although the state second pension will be based on £9,500

- For occupational money purchase schemes (COMPS) and contracted out salary related schemes (COSRS), the position will be more or less the same as under SERPS

9

Tax-free Cash Lump Sums

Most pension funds provide the opportunity to commute part of the pension funds for tax-free cash. There are different rules for different funds. Most financial advisers will tell clients to always take the tax-free cash. The reason for that is that it immediately provides for a diversification of assets. In addition, if an annuity was required, then a voluntarily purchased one using tax-free cash would be more tax efficient than a pension annuity. However, with annuity rates exceptionally low at present, mostly alternative income-producing investments will be used.

Cash may be required to pay off debts, make gifts to family members, pay for that holiday of a lifetime, keeping the business going, university and school fees, refurbishing the house, settling divorce commitments and making investments.

The following pension schemes provide lump sums as follows:

Final salary scheme pension fund/ occupational pension schemes

1. The position after 1.6.1989 is as follows:
   - Maximum tax-free cash is the greater of 3/80ths of final remuneration for each year of service (maximum of 40 years), or 2.25 times the amount of the member's pension before commutation.
   - This is limited to the lesser of 1.5 times final remuneration, or 1.5 times the earnings cap (£145,800 for 2002/03).

2. Final salary pension schemes members between 17.3.1987 and 1.6.1989 are limited to a maximum tax-free lump sum of £150,000 or 1.5 times remuneration, whichever is the lesser (with 20+ years service and where the pension is 2/3 of final remuneration). One can only get maximum lump sum benefits if maximum pension benefits are taken.

3. Final salary schemes members before 17.3.1987 have 1.5 times remuneration without any upper limit. However, they must have 20 years service to get this.

For all of the above there may be different accrual rates dependant on service and other factors (like the pension scheme rules) and advice may be required.

Defined contribution pension schemes, personal pension plans, stakeholder pension plans, group personal pension plans

25% of the accumulated pension fund may be taken as a cash lump sum, free of tax. (but excluding protected rights portion of the fund).

Retirement annuities

3 times the residual annuity may be taken as tax-free cash. This may be higher than the 25% for personal pension plans above. However, if the open market option is used by the annuitant to increase the annuity payable, then the tax-free cash amount reduces to 25%.

It may be tax efficient, if over age 50, to invest into a personal pension plan, obtain tax relief on the contributions and to immediately take the tax-free cash. This cash could again be used for gearing purposes, for example to invest into a tax-reducing VCT (venture capital trust), or even to reduce credit card debt.

10

FURBS – Unapproved Retirement Benefit Schemes

Description

A Funded Unapproved Retirement Benefit Scheme, a FURBS, is an employer contribution scheme, usually for those with earnings in excess of the earnings cap. The earnings cap for 2002/203 is £97,200.

This means that regular pensions contributions can only be made on earnings up to the earnings cap level. Above that level, the employer may contribute to a FURBS (a funded scheme) or an UURBS (an unfounded retirement benefit scheme.)

However, this need not always be the case (only suitable if earnings are above the earnings cap) and cases have been known of FURBS being taken out below the earnings cap. A FURBS enables a high earner to build up alternative investments outside normal pension funding.

Types of scheme

There are two types of unapproved schemes available.

The Funded Unapproved Retirement Benefit Scheme

The employer sets up a trust and makes contributions to the trust, which is for the benefit of the employee. The trust can invest in any type of investment permitted by the scheme, and there are few investment constraints.

The retirement date is flexible and need not be aligned to any other pension scheme's retirement date. Usually, though retirement is by age 75.

The employer's contributions are allowable against profits in the year paid, as expended 'wholly and exclusively for the purposes of trade'.

The employee pays tax on the contribution under Schedule E. The contribution made by the employer is, however, treated as relevant earnings for any exempt approved scheme. This means that FURBS contributions increase your pensionable pay for higher levels of normal pension contributions to other funds.

Employer national insurance is payable on the contributions made.

The main reason why people take out a FURBS is that for a higher rated taxpayer, investment income is taxed at 22%, and UK dividends and interest are taxed at 20%. In addition, capital gains tax is payable at the trust rate of 34%, and capital gains may be deferred and subject to reinvestment reliefs, as well as taper reliefs. Significant tax and investment planning could therefore produce a reasonable investment fund.

The use of offshore funds means that gross roll-up non-distributor investment funds can be used (as tax is only charged when the fund is sold or disposed of) thus further enhancing the investment possibilities.

At retirement, the whole fund can be taken as tax-free cash. Alternatively, an annuity can be taken with the fund proceeds. This would be a voluntary purchase annuity (essentially using your own tax paid capital), with further tax advantages.

FURBS are popular with those wishing to defer their bonus payments into an eventual tax-free cash lump. To avoid NI and also tax on the employer contribution, a discretionary EBT (Employee Benefit Trust) offshore with discretionary payments could be an alternative. However, the FURBS does give a tax-free benefit (the EBT does not); the FURBS designates the employee by name as a beneficiary (he definitely gets the fund); the EBT does not (being discretionary).

Unfunded Unapproved Retirement Benefit Scheme (UURBS)

This is a tax paid scheme. The employer makes a contribution, usually tax relievable, and the employee is taxed on it as income. Employer NI is payable on the contributions.

Essentially, the scheme is a notional one only. It would arise where, for example, the employee has not built up a pension scheme, the employer pays a lump sum and/or a 'pension' to the employee to give the employee a retirement benefit.

Example of a FURBS

Henry is aged 55 and wishes to retire at age 60. He earns in excess of the pensions cap, and is due an annual bonus of £100,000. He does not need the bonus money and would rather defer it to a later date if possible. His employer would, in any event pay NI and he would pay tax if the bonus was paid to him. The bonus payment or the contribution to a FURB would be allowable as a deduction from taxable profits in the employer's hands.

A FURB trust is set up by the employer with Henry as the beneficiary (his family as default beneficiaries), and the £100,000 less the tax payable by Henry is paid into the Trust, where it is invested. Henry pays £40,000 tax and £60,000 is invested. The investment is made into a share portfolio that earns 10% and within the fund is taxed at 20% as UK dividend income. Further contributions are made for a further 4 years on the same basis and same amounts.

Cost to employer: (assuming tax rates stay the same)

Contribution cost:	£100,000 p.a. x 5 years	= £500,000
Employer National Insurance:	£12,800 p.a. x 5 years	= £64,000
Total		£564,000
Less tax allowable of say 30%		(£150,000)
Less NI allowable 30% x £64,000		(£19,200)
Net cost to employer		**£394,800**

Employee Cost:

Tax on contribution at 40% :   £100 000 x 40% x 5 years   = £200,000
Balance of fund invested after tax £60 000 x 5 years   = £390,411
(invested at £5 000 per month at say 10% growth for 5 years)

Employee Benefit:

Compound investment return net of 20% annual tax: £369,833
Tax-free lump sum age 60:   **£369,833**

Why invest in a FURBS over any other investment?

- The employer wants to be seen to be giving additional pension benefits, or top-ups to existing pension schemes.
- The employer may not wish to make contributions to anything else.
- The employee wishes to defer a bonus in a certain investment medium.
- The employer does not have an Employee Benefit Trust (EBT), or the potential tax liability of the EBT payment at a later date suggests that the EBT route is inappropriate.
- The FURB can have tax efficient investments, and can defer capital gains tax as well as taper it.

However, the employee could equally take the bonus, pay the tax, invest into a VCT that grows tax free for three years, and then take a tax-free lump sum. In addition, he would have had tax relief going into the VCT investment and defer a capital gain. However, the VCT investment strategy may not be to his liking, or whether the VCT can realise its investments at the due date and time to pay out may be debatable.

Alternative investments could also be ISAs, Unit Trusts, OEICs and offshore funds with gross roll-up. Self-invested Personal Pension Plans, if not at the pensions cap, could give a tax-free lump sum and a pension scheme and for small amounts if earning under £30,000 p.a. could go into a stakeholder pension scheme (even if you are a member of an occupational pension scheme). However, a FURBS is a generally recognised top-up plan for those above the pensions cap. It may not generally rate as the overall most tax or cost efficient plan, but it does give a tax-free lump sum with no further lock-ins – plus you can decide where to invest your money.

Advantages of FURBS:

- Corporation Tax relief on contributions
- tax-free lump sum payouts on retirement
- retirement date can be variable
- lower investment tax rates on the fund
- wide investment choice
- savings plan for those high earners in excess of the pensions cap
- preferable to EBTs for those wanting absolute certainty, not discretionary payouts.

Disadvantages of FURBS:

- contributions are subject to employee tax under Schedule E
- employer National Insurance is payable on the contributions (but allowable against profits at the rate of corporation tax)
- investment risk, depending on the type of investments used
- charges could vary from one supplier to another
- accounting disclosure required.

11

Partnership Pension Schemes

Partners and partnerships

Partners can be divided into equity partners or salaried partners. **Equity Partners** may contribute to both a personal pension plan or have an occupational pension scheme, such as a SSAS. A **salaried partner** is an employee who may have a profit share, but does not share in the liabilities or debts of the partnership and would not have a capital account. This part deals with equity partners only.

Where partners group themselves together, they could contribute to a small self-administered pension scheme (SSAS). However, there must be twelve or fewer partners to do this. For a larger group, a group personal pension plan is more usual (GPPP). Smaller partnerships may have individual personal pension plans or the older retirement annuity plans, similar to the self-employed.

Partnerships in England and Wales and Northern Ireland are not legal persona as they are in Scotland. In the former, it is the individual members of a partnership who are trading and not the partnership itself.

For taxation purposes, however, income tax for the partners throughout the UK is assessed in the name of the partnership. Partners have been directly assessed from 6th April 1994, when joint assessment was abolished.

Partnerships are governed by the partnership agreement. It is common to find a clause stating that individual partners must provide for their own retirement funding, where there is no partnership pension fund in place. Pension funding is the major method of building wealth outside the business and of making contributions from pre-tax profits.

However, a partnership does not have to have a funded pension scheme. The partnership itself can pay a pension (as an annuity under TA 1988 s. 628 and Revenue Statements of Practice D12 (17/1/75) and SP 1/79) to retiring partners, which has not been pre-funded. Contributions made are tax deductible to the other partners in their partnership proportions. To qualify as earned income for these allowances, the pension (annuity) payable must:

- be paid in accordance with the partnership agreement or supplementary agreement
- not exceed 50% of the average profit of the retiring partner for the best three of the last seven years before retirement
- allow a tax-free cash sum of 25% of the notional accumulated sum to be taken
- be allowed to increase, and where necessary, be paid to a spouse or dependant
- allow 10% of contributions at the percentage level for that age to provide term life assurance cover (previously 5% of net relevant earnings)
- be paid direct or by the purchase of an annuity.

Such a 'fund' may be used for the benefit of the partnership. No loans are allowed if a fund is established, but the fund can purchase commercial property from the partnership and lease it back on commercial terms.

The unfunded pension scheme of annuity payments means that the retiring partner will not be charged to capital gains tax on the capitalised value of the annuity as long as it is regarded as reasonable recognition for past services to the partnership. A reasonable annuity is calculated by taking an average of the partner's best three years assessable profits shares out of the last seven, and then not exceeding the fraction provided in the table below:

Years of service	Fraction per year
1-5	1/60
6	8/60
7	16/60
8	24/60
9	32/60
10 or more	40/60 or (2/3)

Example

Fred Money has been a partner in the legal firm of Level Head and Money for 20 years. In the last seven years, the best three years assessable profits have been £88,675, £127,320, £56,005. The average is therefore £90,667. The annual gross annuity payable to Fred will be 2/3 x £90,667 = £60,444 (net £60,444 – £13,298 (22%) = £47,146)

There are 5 partners in the firm (other than Fred), who will be paying the annuity, and their share is deducted in calculating their taxable income. They deduct basic rate income tax when making the payment and claim relief at the higher rate through their tax returns. Fred pays tax in the normal way on this annuity income. He has received it net of basic rate tax and may have further tax to pay (or reclaim) depending on his personal tax position.

Each partner has gross £12,088 net (12,088 – £2,660) = £9,428 to pay.

Partners may therefore provide for pensions in a tax efficient way without having to set aside capital, if they have left things too late, or merely prefer this course of action. However, their ability to keep up payments in the future must be measured against saving for retirement income through a proper pension fund, rather than relying on a notional one, as outlined above.

Limitations for the unfounded scheme include problems when profits fluctuate, and possibly lower pensions when there has been no funding.

Details of SSAS, Group Personal Pension Schemes (GPPPs), Personal Pension Plans, and Stakeholder schemes are explained elsewhere and are all applicable for equity partners.

Doctors and other qualifying members of the medical profession can contribute to both the NHS pension and to other pension schemes and special rules apply for this.

Salaried partners can be members of their own personal pension plans, or as employees in the partnership scheme for employees, usually a group personal pension plan.

12

Starting a Pension
– What to Do Next

As they say, you're never too young to start! With the advent of stakeholder pensions, the starting age has dropped from 18 to less than age one, and you can contribute without relevant earnings and still get tax relief as pension contributions are now made net of basic rate tax.

You don't even need to contribute to the pension fund yourself – someone else can do it for you, and pension savings are now being made by parents as well as grandparents for children and grandchildren, as investments for the future.

Look at this example. Jim decides that he will contribute the maximum stakeholder pension for his new son Darius of £3,600 gross (£2,808 net). He makes one payment and this is invested at a projected annual compound return of 8% per annum. In fifty years time, this will be worth £168,845.

Alternatively, Joan, age 30, makes a pension payment of £300 per month for 20 years – she will have a fund, if invested at 8% compound per annum, of £196,408. She wishes to retire at age 50, and has made no pension provision.

The steps in the process for starting a pension are:

1. **Decide what level of contribution you can afford to make.**

Even though you may save tax, do not over-stretch yourself. Once a pension contribution has been made, you cannot access the money until the earliest retirement date.

2. Determine your pension plan status.

- If **employed**, and **if your employer does have a pension scheme**, then are you earning above or below £30,000 p.a.?
  - if above, then go the AVC/FSAVC route for your contributions
  - if below, then consider a stakeholder pension scheme, or the AVC/FSAVC route.
- If **your employer has no pension scheme**, then consider a personal pension plan (or stakeholder if contributing below £300 per month gross).
- If **self-employed** then consider a personal pension plan and/or stakeholder variant.
- If a company director or partner, an occupational pension scheme may be considered, such as a SSAS; or a personal pension plan.

3. **Do you have earnings from employment** (net relevant earnings), or earnings such as interest or dividends only? Only stakeholder pension schemes can accept earnings from sources other than employment. Otherwise you may need 'net relevant earnings' to qualify. *Determine your earnings status for type of fund.*

4. **Can your employer contribute to your scheme?** It's worth asking if you set one up – or can you contribute to your employer's scheme? *Determine the extent of who can contribute to your plan and how much.*

5. **Can you make monthly contributions, or do you have single lump sums to invest?** Regular premiums by direct debit ensure that you don't forget to make your contributions. However, it has been cheaper in the past to only make single premium

Pensions Simplified

contributions as the charging structure for regular premiums was higher. Nowadays, many product providers have the same charging structure whether a monthly or single premium. *Determine whether to make regular premium contributions or single premiums, or perhaps both, depending on your circumstances.*

6. **Do you want waiver of premium insurance?** What this means is that, for regular contributions, you can insure against serious illness or disability where you cannot work, and the insurer pays your pension contribution for you. This is not available on stakeholder, but can be a stand-a-lone addition, and is not expensive. PHI schemes also cater for pension premiums if disabled. *Determine whether to have waiver of premium cover, or not.*

7. **What is your investment risk profile?** Do you want a managed investment fund, or options to select from a bigger range of investment opportunities? *Determine how you want your funds invested.*

8. **Do you want to protect your fund** for your heirs and dependants should you die? If employed, you may qualify for death in service benefits, or you may need to insure your own fund. You can also have tax deductible term life insurance. *Determine how much life cover you need, and why.*

9. **Select your normal retirement date.** When you take out a pension plan you would have to choose a date between age 50 and 75.

10. **Select a target pension fund** to aim for. How much must you save over the years for a financially successful retirement? Use the handy calculator elsewhere in the book.

11. **Decide whether to go direct to a pensions provider or whether to use an intermediary financial adviser** to help you with your

selection. Be prepared to pay a fee or commission, depending on your preference. *Choose your plan, going direct or through a financial adviser.*

12. Make sure the plan benefits are **written in trust** to avoid inheritance tax later if you die, and that beneficiaries are determined.

13. Make sure you **keep within the Inland Revenue funding limits**.

14. Set up your plan and make your contributions, then **monitor progress** on a regular basis, to see if you can increase contributions in future years.

The above steps will help you with your planning. As with most things in life, you get out what you put in, so accept responsibility for your own planning and don't leave matters to chance. Through each of these steps, there may be research and analysis to be undertaken; however this is done for you if you use a qualified financial adviser in your preparation.

13

Choices at Retirement – Pensions, Annuities, Draw-down, Phased

There will be a number of choices and options to be considered at retirement and indeed prior to retirement. If a member of a final salary scheme or occupational pension scheme with defined benefits, then the options are less than they would be if a fund had been built up under a personal pension plan for example.

If a member of a defined benefit scheme, the employer/pension trustees will advise on the election options relating to the taking of tax-free cash and the mode of pension payment.

If a member of defined contribution scheme, such as a personal pension scheme, stakeholder, SSAS or group money purchase, then there are a number of distinct options available. Previously, the only choice was to take your tax-free cash and then an annuity. Nowadays, you can take the tax-free cash and defer the annuity for as long as possible – to age 75, when you must take an annuity under present legislation.

The choices include drawing down an income from your fund until retirement date (draw-down), retiring from your pension fund in stages (staggered vesting), deferring a decision (at least to age 75), or taking an annuity. There are also options to insure the fund rather than have the guarantees in the annuities, thus increasing income as well as protecting fund assets. New annuities include those now able to pay surpluses back to your estate on death.

It may be that a number of pension schemes are consolidated at retirement, into say a SIPP – a self-invested personal pension plan, to give greater flexibility, particularly for draw-down.

The benefits of the SIPP route include the flexibility to influence investment decisions, to have flexibility to draw income until annuities have to be taken (currently at age 75), within the Government Actuary's limits. Included in any SIPP analysis would be a Section 32 Buyout Bond for comparison purposes.

Options

a) **Income could be drawn down** until age 75, when an annuity must be purchased (draw-down)

- income available from fund
- tax-free cash available immediately
- minimum income withdrawal is 35% of the maximum
- maximum income also constrained
- flexibility to change income each year within limits
- income escalation could be limited
- after age 65 more risky than an annuity
- investment risk varies according to investment strategy and use of guaranteed funds
- death benefits have three options:
  - return of fund less 35% tax
  - fund balance buys single annuity
  - continue with income withdrawals for 2 years then decide
- all income is taxable as schedule E
- arrange trusts to avoid IHT
- draw-down requires substantial funds and is relatively uncertain
- could deplete pension fund capital
- could apply draw-down to part of the fund, the balance through staggered vesting or phased withdrawals
- flexibility until (maybe) annuity rates improve
- costs of set-up and administration of SIPP inexpensive.

(b) **Pension income could be phased** whereby in each period, a segment of the pension is encashed or vested to provide tax-free cash and an annuity. Both then provide income for the year. The SIPP would have to be segmented to provide this option.

- only use income or capital to meet the need requirements
- segmented balances grow tax free
- tax-free cash may be taken with each segment
- no minimum income
- income depends on the amount vested
- if too high, it could deplete the fund by age 75
- more flexible than draw-down as the whole fund is not committed
- phased annuities can be bought with escalation allowing a mix and match of income types
- maybe risky after age 65 if funds are small – but not in this case
- more volatility is possible if fund values are low and one is forced to encash when unit prices are low – investment strategy will determine investment risk and underlying fund investments
- on death, the full fund could be paid to dependants free of tax
- if the transfer was originally from an occupational scheme, then only 25% is available as cash and the balance must purchase an annuity
- death benefits are better than draw-down
- very tax efficient as tax-free cash is used for income, tax only being paid on the annuity element
- annuities must be purchased for income
- tax-free cash is limited to each encashment period

(c) **Annuities provide a fixed income, which is guaranteed until death.** The pension fund is invested in gilts and fixed interest, or perhaps a with profits annuity, or unit-linked annuity. The fund may provide for a variety of income options, including level income, escalating (at say RPI or 3%), or with profits or unit-linked income (the latter not being certain, but dependant on market conditions).

S

- compulsory purchase annuities' income is taxable (pension funds)
- voluntary purchase annuities' income is partly tax free (from cash)
- no specific minimum or maximum income
- could have highest levels of income payable for life with guarantees
- no income flexibility
- escalation of income possible at say 3%, 5% or RPI
- best suited to risk-averse investors
- pension fund must purchase an annuity by age 75
- no investment risk on conventional annuities
- there is risk with profits or unit-linked annuities (they may not perform)
- death benefits – annuities can be guaranteed for up to 10 years usually
- joint life annuities pay out for two lifetimes
- underlying fund lost on death to the life office
- good health buys an average annuity – poor health a better (impaired) one
- annuities are taxed under schedule E
- voluntary annuities have a tax-free element
- can shop around for the best open-market option annuity

d) **PIPPA class annuities where the guarantees are taken out of the annuity itself, and placed on the fund.**

- better income options
- full original fund returned on death, tax free
- better dependants' benefits
- more flexible options available, e.g. where partner dies before you
- usual increases in income between 20% and up to 100%
- higher income guaranteed for life
- dependants' income partly or wholly tax free if required
- can pass original pension fund value to heirs tax free.

(e) **Annuities returning capital to your estate** were launched in November 2001, but require a minimum fund value of £250,000, and may carry investment risk as funds may be managed within the annuity.

From the above, it can be seen that there are many different options to be considered. The most common annuity-based option (if there are dependants) is usually a joint and survivor annuity, where a pension is payable for two lifetimes, with guarantees of 5 or 10 years (in case the parties die too soon, the annuity continues paying for the guarantee period), level or escalating income (preferable). This is the worse possible option as there is no flexibility with regard to income (particularly if a partner predeceases you), the whole underlying fund is lost on death to the product provider, and annuity rates are at the lowest levels for over ten years. In addition, although the open market option may provide higher income (on average by 11%), the cost of guarantees within annuities accounts for about 65% of the fund value. Income from this source, although guaranteed, will always be very low compared to other sources.

Conceptually, the PIPPA class plan provides the most flexible alternatives, with highest incomes. The full original fund is returned on death, tax free, and the highest income levels can be guaranteed. The costs of guarantees drops from around 65% of the fund value per annum to less than 4% of the fund value per annum, thus ensuring better income.

The guarantees are separately provided, and the client will have to be underwritten for health reasons. Poor health means higher guarantee costs, but then also higher annuity levels through being an impaired life.

Income draw-down is possible, as well as phased retirement with the PIPPA class option, giving maximum flexibility. You must take a view as to the future movement of annuity rates and investment returns when making your decision.

14

Pension Fund Investments

One has a far greater say in the investment strategy and performance of funds under your control, than if an employer or designated fund manager was taking the decisions, or where older pension funds were concerned, when there wasn't very much choice available to you. As a result, pension funds were more often than not invested into managed life office funds, with average or below average returns. Having said that, can you really do better than an experienced fund manager? Some people can, but the vast majority will find it difficult to do so.

Because of the very nature of the pension fund itself, most investment strategy verges on the cautious, and the older you are, and the closer to retirement date you are, the more cautious you become. The last two years have seen great stock-market volatility, where managed funds or tracker funds saw losses of up to 30%. Not many investors can stomach such investment losses, with possibly a few years to go to retirement. It could financially decimate your retirement plans.

Much has to do with the concept of invest risk. The concept has been related to performance or the lack of it on your funds in the past. However, to the retiree, the risk is often of outliving your capital as people retire younger and live longer, rather than the loss of potential investment performance. So, the protection of capital is important, as is its preservation. Pension funds by their nature are conservative investment vehicles, with a mixture of gilts, fixed interest, property and equity investments, as well as cash, making up the bulk of pension fund investments.

One must have a fund investment strategy. This takes into account many different factors and components, and can be changed at any time. One must take into account the risk profile of the pension member(s), their ages, the amount of the contribution made, the size of the fund (larger funds can sustain greater losses than smaller ones), the payouts to be made by the fund in the future (pensions and tax-free lump sums), whether other benefits are to be provided, such as widows' and children's pensions, costs of administration and other factors. Liquidity is a major factor. For example, your pension fund may own the business premises, but at retirement date it must pay you a pension. Must the business premises be sold at that time, and what are the ramifications for doing so?

Modern investment theory is based on the portfolio theory of investment management. This implies the concept of balance. It is a known fact that over a period of time, some investments may have good returns and go up, others may go down in value. Taken together, the balancing should provide a median return as anticipated by the investor. Other theories involve stock picking and charting, as well as the use of derivatives for exceptional returns (and also exceptional falls). Fund managers allow you to move between funds more often at little or no cost, and many pension fund companies invest their funds into better performing vehicles, even with other competing fund managers to obtain superior performance for their clients.

The past few years have seen greater individualisation and diversification amongst pension fund investors, with the advent of the SIPP, the self-invested personal pension plan, for example. Here, the pension fund contributor can select his or her own investments, from a wide range of choices, including individual share selections. Shares from share schemes can even be used as the contribution to the pension fund if required, and qualify for tax reliefs.

Your choices are broadly as follows:

- choose your own funds and investments
- choose a fund manager to make the decisions
- select a managed fund
- select various investment options, usually from managed, with

profits, unit linked, special opportunities, UK equities, global equities, cash, gilts, fixed interest, property and others

- choose a fund supermarket to select a range of investment options in unit and investment trusts, OEICS, and other collective schemes
- allow the pension fund manager discretion to choose the funds to be invested in, according to the risk profile, amount of funds available, size of fund, length to retirement, liquidity and other factors.

It is ultimately your individual choice, because you may not go with a poor performing pension fund product provider, even if you do not personally select the funds. Business owners may opt for a SSAS with wider investment powers, including making loans to the business to purchase capital equipment and machinery, the ability to purchase business premises and other flexible options; or a SIPP to purchase commercial property and hold certain shares. Larger defined benefit and contribution pension schemes will also have a defined investment policy, but this is largely also influenced by the trustees of the fund and the employer. A recent case involved a fund manager being sued for not performing as they said they would (Unilever vs Mercury Asset Management), so fund managers are under great pressure to perform. However, it must be borne in mind that the client accepts a certain investment mix and strategy and often dictates it, and when there is then failure to perform, one can hardly blame the fund manager.

Where individual pension scheme investors are concerned, their risk profile for investment risk must be taken into account. This profile will also change over time, usually becoming more conservative. A fund with a long investment time frame may be more adventurous early on, but within two years of retirement, should be more concerned with protecting and conserving retirement capital, with a more cautious approach adopted.

It is not only pension funds that have an investment strategy need requirement, for annuities are today more flexible, some being unit-linked, others with-profits, and others having an investment mix. This is because like any growth versus fixed interest investments, the likelihood of being ahead over longer terms usually lies with growth investments. Annuities entirely dependent on gilt or fixed interest portfolios will be slow growers, and will merely produce overall falling future incomes. It is for this reason that in a sustained low interest rate environment, the challenge is in how to squeeze more income out of annuities, the investment vehicle for retirement income, compulsory after age 75.

Investment returns on death is also an important feature. Some funds only return premiums paid plus interest at say 4% or 5%, whereas a return of fund is preferred. A recent client example, where a single premium investment was made into a retirement annuity fund 16 years ago, showed a current fund value of £33,456, whereas the return of premiums plus 4% was £2,367, a significant difference. One can ask the life office to change its terms for a small fee. After all, why should your heirs or estate lose the growth on your funds to the product provider if you pass away? The same argument holds for the loss of the underlying annuity funds on death – it is iniquitous that the life office keep such investments – after all they don't just disappear. Times are changing, and these centuries-old practices must also change.

Investment growth does not only apply to the build-up of pension funds. If you go into income draw-down after retirement (until age 75 when you must purchase an annuity), then you also require an investment strategy consistent with providing income, but also for future growth.

Fund management is a highly sophisticated and complex area requiring computer modelling and management where pension fund growth and annuities growth and income provision is required as well as income draw-down. A number of specialist providers offer precisely this type of arrangement when taking out their funds. The fund direction and strategic planning change to suit the individual requirements on a tailor-made basis.

At the actual date of retirement, once you have considered your options, your investments and pension schemes will require decisions to be made to provide you with adequate levels of income and access to capital. If you are investing for income or capital growth, there is a wide range of investments to choose from, depending on your risk profile and the type of investment required. You will also take other factors into account, such as tax efficiency, investment protection, and the investment risk inherent in the investment itself.

At the actual date of retirement, you will have investments already in place, and new investments to be considered for your tax-free lump sums, as well as an investment strategy for your underlying pensions schemes if you are deferring a pension to a later date.

The investment process in retirement will be more concerned with ensuring that your retirement income remains adequate and that your investments are properly managed. Ensure that investments do not become obsolete over time and are performing as well as can be expected.

Be prepared to regularly review your investments in retirement and change your investment strategy if your circumstances change. This could be to develop a strategy not to lose investment value because of inheritance taxes, as well as to provide for long-term care, as an eventuality.

When heirs and dependants inherit from you, the process of investment and the investment cycle will begin anew. Younger people with a long span to go to retirement will invest your older money for adventurous growth, and take risks with it, totally contrary to what you had done over the past ten to twenty years.

15

Cost of Delay in Taking Out a Pension Scheme

One must begin the pension funding process as soon as possible to avoid the cost of delay. With long-term funding plans, the sooner you begin, the lighter the monthly investment load or burden to be undertaken. The cost of delay is the loss or reduction of final fund benefits (what could have been, had you started earlier), and what that might mean to you, in terms of reduced income.

By examining the table below, you will see the impact at various ages on the eventual fund value, by delaying by only one year the beginning of your investment funding plan.

Cost of Delay – Eventual fund value lost by delaying further provision by only one year at different ages. Assume that the retirement date is age 65

Delay period	% loss of benefit – retire at age 65
from age 21 to 22	10%
from age 31 to 32	15%
from age 41 to 42	16%
from age 51 to 52	18%
from age 61 to 62	38%

As you can see, by merely delaying the beginning of the funding of your investment plan by one year, at various periods in your life, a significant negative impact is made on your eventual fund value. The impact is much higher, the longer you delay.

Example

Fanny has decided at age 21 to delay the funding of her pension fund by one year. She was going to invest £1,000 a year into pension funding. That £1,000 delay will cost Fanny 10% of the value of her final pension fund at age 65. To prove it, take £1,000 and invest it at, say, 10% compound interest for 44 years and also 43 years. At a term of 43 years: £60,240 is the fund value. At a term of 44 years, the fund is worth £66,265, a difference of £6,024, or 10% more. That 10% of fund could buy you an income for life, which you now won't have. Think about it.

The target funding figures should also adjust. For example, because you didn't fund £1,000 at age 21, you should have to now fund more than £1,000 at age 22 to make up the difference, if you want the same end fund benefit. That is why at age 61, the difference is 38%, because the loss of a year when so close to age 65 means considerable funding is required because of the delay by one year, and the ground that has to be made up.

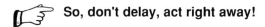 **So, don't delay, act right away!**

16

Pension Rights

The past decade has seen a surge in pensions legislation largely resulting from European directives, but also from appellate division cases and cases heard at the European Courts of Justice and Human Rights at Strasbourg.

There has also been greater awareness and protections offered with regard to pensions schemes, as a result of the fraud perpetrated by Robert Maxwell on the Mirror and other pension funds, the pensions mis-selling debacle of the late eighties and early nineties, where people were transferred from perfectly good final salary schemes into personal pension arrangements, and now companies having to reflect final salary schemes on their balance sheets – something that could affect their profits, if the scheme is not properly funded. Pension scheme liabilities are such that trustees could be held personally responsible with unlimited liability and directors of company pension schemes could go to gaol if schemes are not properly and adequately funded.

Final salary schemes are subject to a minimum funding requirement (MFR). Schemes must be 100% funded, and if not, must put funding schedules in place over the next five years. Limited Pension Increases must be granted on all benefits and no surpluses may be paid to employers until this has been done. Members can expect at least an escalation of pension benefits at the LPI, which is the RPI capped at 5% per annum.

Sexual equality is ensured since the Barber v Guardian Royal Exchange case in 1990, requires men and women to receive equal pay for equal work and defines pay as including a benefit from a company pension scheme. Mr Barber could now receive a redundancy benefit similar to that a woman might receive (he was getting less) in the same situation. However, this is only applicable to post-1990 schemes and other cases followed to bring about sexual equality in pension schemes. This means no discrimination on differing pension ages, and equality of pension provision for men and women. Occupational pension schemes must give equal access to benefits as well as equal benefits, and this is now proving to also be the case for part-timers.

In the European case of Bilka-Kaufhaus in 1986 it was found that employees could not be excluded from an occupational pension scheme if that discrimination was indirect and on the grounds of being a part-time worker. Part-timers can demand to belong to a pension scheme, so long as they pay their share of the pension contributions, and admission to the scheme can be back-dated to 1976. These actions have clarified the rights of workers, but will be costly for employers, especially those with large part-time work forces.

Since 6th April 1988, employees have the right not to join an employer's pension scheme or to remain members of it. If they do leave, they are under no obligation to join any other scheme and the employer does not have to contribute to it if they do so.

Employee members must have pension scheme information disclosed to them, which includes an annual report and actuarial valuation.

Whilst almost all of the case law and legislation has been around occupational pension schemes, the principles have been taken on board for all other pension arrangements with regard to equality of benefits, and no sexual discrimination on pension benefits. So much so, that it looks like unisex annuity rates are becoming more common, which will probably mean lower annuity rates in the future, as females are usually rated down because they live five years longer than men, on average.

It has also spawned new pensions instruments, such as the stakeholder pension, the first of many to meet the CAT standard kitemark on costs and transparency with regard to values and charging structures. For example, there is a 1% charging structure limit. That means real value for money for pension policy owners, hitherto with vastly decreased values due to charges and commissions. Already the filtering process has begun with some product providers adopting the processes across other products, and enabling fees to be charged for work done for clients as opposed to high commissions. As far as pension rights are concerned, one can now insist on better values and receive better products. The complaints procedures are quick to address or redress situations where there has been mis-selling or other misdemeanors, and pensions law and practice is very tightly regulated and controlled now.

We have tight compliance on the one hand, but an opening up of individual investment opportunity on the other, with the new 'defined contribution regime' allowing members to enjoy the benefits of defined contribution schemes (like stakeholder pensions), whilst also experiencing the benefits from a defined benefits scheme (like an occupational final salary scheme).

There are further protections offered within the pension schemes themselves. For example, group money purchase and personal pension schemes that have contracted out under the Social Security Act 1986 will have protected rights separately identified to ensure that the corresponding fund is used to purchase prescribed benefits at age 60. (However no tax-free cash is allowable from protected rights funds.)

One area that has vexed pension scheme members in the past has been in relation to bankruptcy and the protection offered to pension benefits. The general rule is that occupational pension schemes are safe and their assets cannot be attached. Personal pension schemes may be a different matter. Usually if aged over 50, the trustee in bankruptcy has forced retirement to attach the tax-free lump sum, as well as the pension payments that flow from the fund. Pension assets could also be attached if contributions had been made in fraud of creditors.

Where pension rights are concerned, you have the right to belong to a scheme or not, to make contributions as best you can, and to be treated fairly and equally, both as a worker and also as a member of a pension scheme. It is your right to take up a pension scheme, and to contribute to it, even if you have no relevant earnings, and are a babe in arms. You have the right to make representations to pension fund trustees and to receive certain reports and accounts and to question how a scheme is being run or even invested. Some of the rights are common law ones, others flow from case law and statute. You have the right to have your pension fund protected from others, including your employer and unscrupulous salespeople who may have misadvised you to your detriment, and you may even have a right to compensation if you have lost value or pension benefits.

17

Pension Transfers and Opt Outs

If you are moving jobs, you may have to transfer from an existing pension scheme with your old employer to the new employer's pension scheme, or set up your own scheme if you become self-employed. You may even decide that pension schemes are not for you and wish to opt out of your current employer's scheme, or think you can do better by setting up your own pension fund. Some people may not like the 'lock-in' nature of pension schemes and try to transfer their funds to another country or pensions regime where maybe they can enjoy better cash benefits. There are many reasons for wanting to transfer pension benefits or to opt out of their present arrangements, and some of these aspects are covered below. Comment was made in the previous chapter with regard to opting out, and this chapter focuses on the various reasons for making a transfer from one fund to another.

Transferring from one employer to another

The pension fund trustees and administrators must give you a transfer value. This is usually less than the current value of the pension scheme, but some schemes offer the current fund value to transfer. Others, charge a penalty to move funds.

If moving jobs, then you have the choice of leaving your pension benefits and funds where they are and making them 'paid up'. At retirement date, you will then enjoy reduced benefits for your service to the time of leaving.

If leaving an occupational pension scheme, then you should receive a 'leaving service benefits statement' which must be produced within two months of leaving. This will give you various options.

You would have the option of a refund of contributions made. If you leave with less than two years qualifying service, a refund of your own contributions may be made (but not the employer's), with 20% tax deducted from the payment made.

If you leave without the refund of contributions, then your benefits are preserved in the occupational pension scheme, unless you wish to transfer a value to another fund. Preserved benefits are usually paid out as a deferred pension at normal retirement date, based on your years service to date of leaving. If you left after 1st January 1991, the deferred pension will be revalued on the basis of the lower of the RPI or 5% per annum compound up to the year before normal retirement date.

If you were a member of a money purchase (defined contribution) scheme, then the investment yield or bonuses must accrue and be applied at the same rate as existing members would have, towards your final benefits.

If you have left your employer after 1st January 1986, then if entitled to preserved benefits, you would acquire a right to a cash equivalent which is called the transfer value.

This must be used as follows:

- to buy additional rights in another approved occupational pension scheme
- a single premium transfer to a section 32 buy out policy to buy a policy from another pension provider
- a single premium to a personal pension scheme or a stakeholder pensions scheme from another pension provider.

A transfer value analysis should enable you to make decisions as to the best possible option for you. If you left the fund with the old employer, a major consideration is whether that scheme would offer pension increases to you. Also, if it was a contracted out pension scheme (contracted out of SERPS), then there would be a need to provide for a GMP (guaranteed minimum pension) under a section 32 policy, or to provide for protected rights under a personal pension scheme.

If you were a member of a personal occupational pension scheme, such as an EPP (Executive personal pension plan), as opposed to a grouped occupational scheme, then it may be possible to transfer the scheme to a new employer, but new Inland Revenue approval is required, and note that the new employer does not have to take it on. There may also be issues with years service in working out the benefits, but this is usually treated as continuous.

Transferring from an employer to a self-employed scheme

The same options and considerations need to be taken into account as above. However, as a self-employed individual, you may only have a personal pension plan or a stakeholder plan. There is no problem in transferring fund values from an occupational pension scheme to a personal pension plan, but note the comments on the possibility of having to provide for a GMP through a section 32 buy-out contract rather than a personal pension plan. You would have to analyse the position carefully and take all factors into account. You could leave the scheme where it is, or make the transfer.

Pension transfers and opt outs are complicated issues, and professional advice may be required before acting.

Transfers at retirement date

Retirement is a time of consolidation of pension funds and the implementation of options. It is possible to transfer from an occupational pension scheme to a personal pension scheme before retirement and then to retire from the latter. The reasons for doing so may include better pension benefits, particularly if medically impaired and much higher annuity rates are available than the occupational pension scheme which does not take these factors into account (being purely a mechanical process based on years' service and final salary).

In addition, you may get better death benefits as well as dependants' benefits through making the transfer. Occupational schemes usually don't pay benefits to anyone other than a widow or widower, so a divorced ex-spouse whom you wish to benefit may not benefit, or another third party. By moving your scheme in this way, on your death other parties may benefit.

You may also wish to consolidate your retirement annuity funds. Income draw-down does not apply to retirement annuities, so a transfer to a personal pension scheme of the retirement annuity funds would facilitate this. Similarly with using the open market option – a transfer must first be made to a personal pension plan to do this. Significant higher annuity benefits may be achieved through the open market option, but also higher rates may be offered for larger funds being placed with annuity providers.

The same applies to a consolidation of personal pension plans to mature at the same age if required or for better deals, impaired life quotes and annuity purchase. Bear in mind though that some retirement annuities and personal pension plans may have high level annuity guarantees and perhaps one would get a better deal by staying with the existing product provider than using the open market option, and the situation needs to be carefully analysed in each case.

Transfers may also be in the client's interests to achieve higher death benefits, especially where the death benefits are a return of premiums plus, say, 4% as opposed to a return of fund. Watch, however, the effect on contribution funding and the value of tax-free cash levels, especially with retirement annuities with longer than average terms.

Early retirement

If you wish to retire early, then a penalty factor will be applied, the amount of which depends on the rules of your pension fund. You could be better off by making a fund transfer first, rather than by retiring early from an existing occupational scheme.

18

A Pension for Your Spouse and Family Members

There are a number of different pension options when considering how to provide a pension for one's spouse or partner or family members.

Using your spouse or partner in the business can save you thousands of pounds, but also help by boosting retirement and pension funding significantly. Ensure that your spouse has an employment contract if an employee, or is included in the partnership agreement, if a partner.

Salaries paid to partners or spouses are tax deductible, and, at lower limits, no national insurance contributions are payable. The first £4,615 as the personal allowance in 2002/03 is not taxable, and by creating another taxpayer with lower tax rates, can save money all around. It also helps to get the housekeeping tax deductible!

Pension planning should involve the family unit and not be the sole preserve of perhaps one partner only. There is tremendous scope for pension contributions by the business as well as individually.

Firstly, the introduction of the Stakeholder pension scheme has opened a number of doors, in that no 'net relevant earnings' are required. Anyone, as well as the employer, can contribute to a stakeholder pension for a spouse or family member. The maximum annual contribution is £3,600 gross with a net payment of £2,808 being made (net of the 22% rate of basic rate tax).

At retirement date, which must be between ages 50 and 75, a tax-free lump sum of 25% of the fund can be taken and a reduced pension, or a larger pension and no tax-free cash. The pension or annuity is taxable.

If the spouse or partner has earnings, then a personal pension plan contribution can be made based on a percentage contribution level as at the age attained. For example, if below age 35 at the 5th April, then 17.5% of net relevant earnings can be contributed to a personal pension plan. The contribution made is tax relievable and no NIC is payable on pension contributions. The treatment at retirement is similar to stakeholder pensions mentioned above.

If the spouse or partner is employed, then an Executive pension plan (EPP) can be offered with single premiums payable, or monthly regular contributions, or a combination of both. Funding limits are generous, and actuarially based on age, years to retirement and salary. The following example shows this.

Married male or female retiring at age 60, salary £3,432 per annum

Present age	Annual Current Funding	% of salary
25	£892	26%
40	£1,750	51%
50	£3,809	111%
55	£7,928	231%

The level of earnings as an employee is below the national insurance level, and no income tax is payable, because the earnings are below the personal allowances level. The business can pension these tax-free earnings, at a substantial level. The contributions paid by the business are tax deductible. At retirement date, the normal rules for an occupational pension scheme apply.

Your spouse or partner could become a partner in your business, and make contributions to a personal pension scheme, or be a member of an occupational scheme such as a SSAS, where the business contributes for him or her. Obviously, income or profit share must be proven to participate.

You may even have a combination of schemes and arrangements. For example, you may have the stakeholder and also the EPP, provided earnings are £30,000 and below.

There are many different ways to ensure that your spouse or partner, and indeed other family members, benefit from having their own pension funding and the financial security that comes with it. It is also beneficial in that the housekeeping, usually paid out of after tax income, can be made into a tax deductible item, and can provide a firm basis for pension funding.

Importantly also is the fact that retirement planning encompasses all family members, who can contribute to it. This ultimately lessens the strain for the main breadwinner, and provides financial independence for the other parties.

19

Tax Implications of Pension Schemes

The general rules are as follows, for pension schemes, pensions, annuities, and tax-free lump sums.

Inland Revenue approved pension funds

Contributions

Contributions to the pension scheme are tax relievable within Inland Revenue limits. The level of contributions and tax relief is determined by the type of pension scheme you have, your age, sex, income that qualifies, whether the scheme is a personal one or owned by the employer; actuarial determinations and investment performance affect future funding on some schemes; costs are also a major factor.

Occupational pension schemes (owned by the employer)

Defined Benefits Schemes: Contributions are set by the actuary

Defined Contribution Schemes: Contributions are determined by the employer, ultimately, with the advice of the actuary

Contributions reduce the employer's taxable income.
There is no national insurance payable on contributions.

Personal pension schemes (owned by the individual)

Personal Pension Schemes: Contributions are set by a formula, based on 'net relevant earnings' and a percentage of those earnings, as follows:

Ages between	% Contribution
Any Age	£3,600 and no earnings required
Under 36	17.5% of net relevant earnings
36-45	20%
46-50	25%
51-55	30%
56-60	35%
61-74	40%

Stakeholder pension scheme contributions need not be based on 'net relevant earnings' and £300 per month or £3,600 p.a. gross can be made. Contributions are always made net (£2,808) of basic rate tax.

Contributions to approved exempt pension schemes are tax deductible, either individually or corporately.

Contributions made to an unapproved pension scheme, such as a FURB are also deductible, but taxable in the hands of the individual, as income.

Pensions and annuity payments

Pension and annuity payments from compulsory purchase pension funds are taxable in the hands of the recipient.

Tax-free lump sums

A proportion of the pension fund may be commuted as a tax-free cash lump sum payment.

For personal pension schemes and stakeholder plans, 25% of the fund is tax free. Pensions cap limits apply.

For retirement annuities, the tax-free lump sum is a calculation made as 3 times the annual pension before commutation. Pensions cap limits do not apply.

85

For retirement annuities transferred to personal pension plans for the open market option, then the tax-free lump sum is 25% of the fund value. Pensions cap limits apply.

For occupational pension schemes, including SSAS, EPP, defined benefit and defined contribution occupational pension schemes, Inland Revenue rules apply.

Pre 1987 schemes: 1.5 x final remuneration after 20 years service (with many caveats) There is no cash limit (i.e. no pensions cap)

Post 1987 schemes: 2.25 x the initial annual rate of pension before commutation (including the value of AVCs and FSAVCs), or 3/80ths x final salary for each year of service up to a maximum of 40 years service, whichever is the greater. Therefore one cannot have more than 1.5 times final salary as a lump sum.

Tax-free lump sums are limited by the pensions cap which is £97,200 in 2002/03. Thus, 1.5 x £97,200 = £145,800 is the maximum tax-free cash.

FURBS – tax-free cash

The whole of a FURBS pays out tax-free cash without limit.

The Pension Fund itself

The growth within the approved exempt pension fund is not subject to capital gains tax, income tax, or corporation tax. If assets are sold, there is no capital gains tax payable.

Furbs

Tax is payable on investment (savings) at 20% and dividend income at 22%. This is because the fund is not approved nor exempt.

The above gives a brief overview of the various tax implications with regard to pension funds, whether approved or unapproved.

20

Fee-based Financial and Retirement Planning

Financial planners charge fees for advice. Brokerage or commission is usually paid as part of the product implementation process. Both advice and implementation functions can be time-costed, and commissions arising could be rebated back into the product purchased, or to the individual or business to whom the product sale is made.

The two questions probably uppermost in the minds of readers are whether it is worth paying a fee for financial planning advice, and how do you assess the adviser and the quality of the advice to be given? These are difficult questions, especially as many pensions specialists are good at choosing the right kind of funds for you to invest in, but when it comes to actual retirement and the various options open to them for their clients, are sadly lacking.

Associations like the Institute of Financial Planning (based in Bristol) have been pushing fee-based financial planning for years, and have a register of certified financial planners. So does SOFA, the Society of Financial Advisers, and financial planners at the LIA, the Life Assurance Association. Those with the CFP, the certified financial planner status would probably be your best bet. Retirement planning, after all, does not only mean dealing with your various pension plans, but encompasses a whole range of investment planning, savings, and ongoing life assurance.

Long-term care possibilities need to be taken into account, and if in business, it may even mean succession planning for the business and other factors. Estate planning and tax planning also form an intrinsic part of the advice process and need to be taken into account. The move in the financial services industry is that if advice is to be independent, it must be fee based, allowing the client to make his or her own judgment call on what products to select, and whether to use the same advisers or not for later products or services. Others are content to have commission-based advice (as they don't like paying fees), or to have commission offset fee-based advice (which is most common). However, the preferred route is that fees are for advice, and commissions are payable for the implementation of that advice, if required (or further fees are payable). Both functions require time-costed work to be spent on behalf of the client, and at the end of the day, the process costs must be accounted for.

The average level of fees for a senior financial planner would be in the range of £100 – £125 per hour, and an initial report could cost between £750 and £1,500 depending on the complexity involved. As retirement planning is a process that may take many months or years, some prefer to pay a monthly retainer for ongoing advice.

The typical retirement planning advice process would be as follows:

1. Meeting with client to establish objectives.
2. Client instructions drawn up from the objectives.
3. Terms of Business completed, agreeing to fees or other payment structures. (No advice may be given until Terms of Business are agreed).
4. Data gathering phase, and fact finding, risk profiling.
5. Restatement of objectives and prioritisation in order of importance
6. Research and analysis – existing product details and product provider liaison.
7. Initial report completed.
8. Testing of report suggestions and recommendations.
9. Second report or tiered reporting structure with file notes.
10. Product and service research and analysis, including investments, annuities, further pensions, long term care, estate

and inheritance tax planning, wills, life assurance, debt management and personal development.
11. Examination of proposals and key features documentation relating to products and their selection.
12. Implementation of the agreed plan.
13. Monitoring, feedback and follow-up.
14. Restatement of objectives and further report to keep on track.

It is not widely known among prospective clients, exactly what processes are involved in successful financial planning, nor the various compliance features that have to be complied with. The above gives some idea of the processes involved. Without this information, you may think the following merely occurs:

1. meeting with client
2. data gathering
3. presentation of report or 'reasons why' letter
4. you get sold something.

The biggest decisions in your life are made at retirement. A mistake at this stage could spell a financial disaster. You may only have one pension fund, and one tax-free lump sum and if you make the wrong decisions, you have to live with them for the rest of your life.

For example, you may decide at retirement (as you are married or have a partner), that the sensible thing to do is to have a pension or annuity that gives you a pension whilst alive, and then pays a (reduced) pension to your spouse or partner. You want the pension to escalate annually to keep up with the cost of living (at say 3% or the RPI); if both of you die too soon, you want the pension fund to continue for at least a guaranteed period of certainty (payable to dependants or heirs). You feel you could invest a tax-free lump sum better and it also gives you financial control to do so. At retirement, your risk profile changes to more cautious, as you cannot afford to lose your money. You are concerned that you may outlive your money, and may become a 'hoarder' and spendthrift. Typical of most people, isn't it? Sure, because it makes sense to think in this way.

You are also concerned that you may or will lose your entire pension fund value if you die, and it cannot be passed on to your heirs or dependants.

What most people do (well, about 95% of them) is follow the instructions from the product provider on how to purchase their pension or annuity (or if employed, merely accept the pension details from their employer), and certainly for the former, maybe in the wrong type of arrangement, unsuited to their retirement needs. In other words, the advice you get may not be the right advice. What may seem to be perfectly normal to you (to take a pension for yourself and your spouse, with escalating income and guarantees) could also be an inflexible option. For example, if your partner dies before you, you will be locked into a low-level pension for the rest of your life; whereas what you may want is the ability to increase income in retirement, to have your whole original pension fund pay out on death – instead of losing it – tax free. Don't merely accept the options given by the product provider. Always ensure that every alternative has been properly thought out before making those all-important decisions.

For example, what if your spouse or partner dies before you? Bad luck, you are still locked in to that annuity rate chosen at the outset to pay for two lifetimes, even though it will now only pay out for one lifetime. Do you have any flexibility or control at all? Not much. You may select a draw-down option, but eventually you must buy an annuity (at age 75). Have you protected your pension fund value for your heirs? Not likely, as you didn't think it could be done. Have you got the best deal at retirement? Are you a smoker? That last statement could increase your pension annuity payments. Has the whole market place been researched to get you the best open market option, or impaired annuity option? You could significantly increase your income in retirement, and create new lump sums at the same time – if only you knew how.

The pension process described above (two pensions, escalating, paying out for a term certain etc) is the most expensive and inflexible option. The guarantees to be taken out of the pension fund to pay for that 'normal' option can take up to 70% of your fund value, leaving the rest to buy you an income. Modern retirement planning techniques financially engineer you the best deal from your money. You *can* get a higher income, you *can* protect your funds for your heirs, you *can* make the process more flexible, with more options, if correctly advised.

The amount of any fees to be paid, in reality, pales into insignificance, if you are receiving the best retirement and financial planning advice. Everyone, no matter how small they feel their retirement funds are, can improve their positions through proper financial planning.

Our strategies for people entering the actual retirement cycle is to keep them as flexible as possible, as big changes are on the way, following announcements made by the Treasury early in 2002 . This will mostly affect the present rigid structure of annuities and how to make them more flexible.

21

Death before Retirement

Should you die 'in service', in other words before retirement, then the pension fund rules will usually stipulate what sort of death benefits are payable and when.

Employers may have death in service benefits, arising from the pension fund itself, or provided by group scheme life assurance. The latter is usually available up to retirement age and then ceases. Group life cover is a multiple of salary, for example two or four times final remuneration, or a fixed amount, and is payable to named beneficiaries or dependants. Payments made by the trustees, for tax reasons, are always discretionary , but a letter of wishes is followed, giving direction for lump sum payments.

If there are no additional group scheme or death in service benefits, then on death before retirement, there would either be a return of current fund value (the better deal), or a return of contributions paid plus say 4% or 5% (worse than a return of current fund value). The differences can be enormous, especially where single premium contributions have been made – as much as 80% less than current fund values. One can approach the pension provider and ask for a change in how and what death benefits are payable – naturally for a charge to make this change.

Such payments on death before retirement are usually tax free. However, some partnership group life schemes may provide tax-free benefits on the first death, but taxable death benefits thereafter, depending on how the scheme was set up in the first place.

22

Death after Retirement

Once you have retired from your pension fund, you will be receiving your monthly pension or annuity. Your pension funds will have been invested by the pensions provider to produce an income, and this is generally known as an annuity income. Unless there is a guarantee operating, the pension itself will come to an end.

The type of death benefits, if any, will depend on the type of annuity or pensions contract, or other arrangement in force at the time.

The most common types are as follows:

Occupational pension schemes

If single, the pension will merely cease. Some schemes have a guaranteed period of payment, and pension payments will continue to the estate of the deceased, or nominated beneficiary or dependant.

If married, usually a reduced pension is payable to the spouse, until his or her death, depending on the scheme rules. 50% widow's or widower's pensions are common, but the range could be from less than that to up to 2/3 of the member's pension.

Personal pension schemes and schemes where annuities are payable

Much depends on the type of the scheme. A scheme with a term certain guarantee will pay out for that term and then cease. For example, if the annuity is payable for two lifetimes, but for a minimum of 10 years, and both annuitants die in, say, year eight, then the annuity continues paying for another two years (to the estate or dependants) before it ceases.

If a **single life annuity**, then after any guaranteed period, the annuity will cease paying.

If a **joint and survivor annuity**, then on the first death, the annuity continues paying to the survivor (usually a reduced amount) until the death of the survivor, when it ceases – unless within the term certain guarantee period, if there is one attached. If the spouse dies before the member, then on the death of the member, the annuity will cease unless within a term certain guarantee period.

If a **single life nil guarantee annuity** is taken, for the highest income option, and the underlying pension **fund is insured**, then on the death of the annuitant, the annuity itself ceases, but the insurance proceeds pays out in trust outside of the deceased's estate, free of all taxes. This may then be reinvested for income, or a voluntary purchase annuity which is tax efficient.

If the situation is a fund **in income draw-down**, then the following occurs. There are three options for the spouse under draw-down:

1   A return of fund less 35% tax – there is no inheritance tax payable unless it is left to the estate. The option must be taken up within two years of the deceased passing away.

2   The remaining fund buys a single annuity. If the spouse inheriting the pension fund then dies, the fund can be passed on to heirs.

3   To continue with income withdrawal for two years before options (i) or (ii) above. To continue to receive an income until the policyholder would have turned age 75, or the dependant's 75th birthday if sooner. Dependant children under age 18 can also benefit.

If the funds have **been phased**, then the position is as follows. On death, the full fund can be paid to dependants free of tax. If the transfer was originally from a company scheme, then only 25% may be taken as tax-free cash and the balance as an annuity. The death benefits are better than draw-down. One can also purchase an impaired life annuity, if required.

It is unlikely that any death after retirement life cover benefits will be available, unless provided independently by the annuitant.

In most instances, it would be in the interests of all parties to have death benefits paid in trust outside of the estate, to avoid probate before being paid out to beneficiaries.

23

Long-term Care

Long-term care will affect 25% of those over age 80, and is an aspect not properly provided for by retirees. A physical or mental disability could occur at any time, and care may need to be provided in a nursing home or 'in the community' at your own home.

The costs of long-term care could financially cripple a retiree, leaving his or her dependants destitute, and using up income and capital to such an extent that nothing is left for one's heirs. The average costs of proper care could run to about £2,000 per month, more if acute hospital care is required.

If you wish the State to pay for care, then you need to have qualifying assets of no more than £19,000. You get limited support with assets between £11,750 and £19,000. Below £11,750, you qualify for full support, within limits. The means test includes income. You first have to use up your own assets and income, before the State, through the local authorities and Department of Work and Pensions pays for you. You could stay in your house, but when you die, it could be sold to pay for long-term care costs. Over 40,000 homes are sold each year, because of this situation.

It is therefore vital that your retirement planning includes planning at all stages of retirement, including the possibility of going into care. The position is worsened if you have to care for an elderly relative. Without adequate lifetime pension and investment funding, savings and long-term care plans become prohibitively more expensive the older you get. As with many people then, you may need more money as you get older, not less.

Long-term care insurance is a fairly recent innovation in the UK market place. It will provide funds to pay for nursing care when you cannot look after yourself, and fail a number of Activities of Daily Living (ADL) tests.

Some policies provide pure insurance, others are investment based, and they are to be found both offshore and in the UK. To claim insurance benefits, the individual must usually be incapable of performing two or three out of five or six ADLs, such as bathing, dressing or feeding oneself. Where the policy proceeds are paid directly to the care provider, then these benefits are tax free.

Policies can be funded on either a lump sum or a regular premium basis. Some contracts are structured as investments and if no claim is made during the policyholder's lifetime, then the fund is returned. There is no tax relief on the premiums, and the policy may not cover acute conditions (such as major surgery) or some mental illnesses that are difficult to prove.

The Government appointed a Royal Commission that reported in March 1999, and came out strongly in advising people to fund for long-term care. The view appears to be that the Government will fund care but not residential costs in the future, but still has a long way to go. The State means-tested capital limits were increased from 8 April 2002. The State will meet the full costs of care where assets in total are less than £11,750 in value and proportionate costs where assets are valued at between £11,750 and £19,000. There is no State assistance where assets exceed £19,000. These assets do not include the value of your house, but your house can be sold after you die, if no dependant is living in it. Income and capital assessed include everything you have – pensions, most state benefits, savings, investments and possibly your home.

One of your strategies may be to sell the house and to invest the cash to provide for income whilst in care, with a return of the investment to your heirs or dependants on your death. Other planning would involve getting your income and capital into exempt areas. For example, qualifying capital includes property, shares and cash, but not capital held by a discretionary trust. However, one must be careful not to deprive oneself of certain assets, as the authorities could add this back in assessing you.

The **main capital to be disregarded** for the long-term care assessment is as follows:

- the surrender value of a life policy
- the value of one residence under certain circumstances
- proceeds of the sale of any premises formerly occupied
- future interest in property other than in certain land and premises
- gifts in kind from a charity
- personal possessions, including works of art
- certain business assets
- capital not in your name (only your share of a joint bank account can be included)
- certain rights that have not yet crystallised as cash but would have a value to a third party

The **main income disregards** are as follows:

- income from disregarded capital assets
- income support payments
- income from an annuity
- from personal injury trusts
- from a life interest or life rent
- earnings from outside the UK
- tax payable
- expenses from voluntary or charitable bodies
- up to 50% of your occupational pension if not residing with your spouse or maintaining him or her
- payments by third parties to your living costs
- any income in kind
- certain payments from insurance policies
- council tax benefits
- income support for housing costs
- many other exemptions

Planning areas would be to invest in qualifying life policies (providing for long-term care if required), planning around the house, transferring assets to heirs, planning with trusts. However, the wealthy will battle to shelter every conceivable asset, and the better view is to rather utilise all assets to pay for care, thus ensuring private not State care as being better for you.

24

Pensions and Divorce

Divorce happens to a third of the general population at any one time, and pensions have become an important part of the divorce settlement. This is particularly the case where, for example one spouse worked and made 'net relevant earnings' for pension scheme contributions, or enjoyed an occupational pension scheme and its benefits and the other spouse brought up the family, and was unable to be in the workplace.

Not only did that spouse rely on his or her partner for income during their working lifetimes, but also for retirement income. Problems were then bound to arise in the event of divorce, as to how the pension fund was to be shared, if at all. The sharing aspect being a difficult proposition may not have been entirely the fault of the member of the pension scheme, though. The rules of the pension fund often meant that pension assets were not divisible for non-contributory, non-pension fund members, and that pension funds before retirement could not be attached for divorce purposes. In addition, the Inland Revenue rules were such that membership of a pension fund approved by the Inland Revenue, could only be possible under a given set of criteria, and that one who had not satisfied these rules could not own the pension fund. Therefore, the non-income-earning spouse could not share in the fund prior to retirement.

After retirement had taken place, the situation was completely different. It was not a retirement fund in place, but rather a stream of income and that could be attached by the courts. However, the retiree would still have full use of the tax-free lump sum, and also the decision whether to take it or not in the first place. If divorce was being contemplated, the likelihood of a full pension without a tax-free lump sum was a distinct possibly – to deny the other party access to the tax-free lump sum.

The divorcing parties would also still be bound to each other after the divorce had taken place, as the income would be split after the divorce. Divorce reformers favoured a clean break and settlement, and the only way forward was to divide the pension scheme assets before retirement and allow pensions to be taken with each portion, separately.

The other major area of concern had been the fact that a divorced spouse was no longer a widow of the deceased pension member and would lose valuable pension benefits if the member died. This was particularly the case when the member remarried or left letters of wishes for the payment of funds to others.

The Welfare Reform and Pensions Act 1999 enabled pensions splitting to occur from 1 December 2000 when divorce settlements are contemplated.

Under a pension splitting or sharing order, there would be a pension debit (a reduction in the value of the pension holder's fund), and a pensions credit in the hands of the former spouse. If a money purchase fund, the value of the fund would be reduced by the pension debit. An occupational pension scheme may create a new member's category to cover a former spouse, who then becomes a member of the pension scheme in his or her own right. If a final salary scheme, the credit and debit would have to be revalued through to the date of retirement.

Where valuations are concerned, the basis for determining how much the pension credit or debit would be worth is the cash equivalent transfer value, or any other such value as agreed by the Court.

If before retirement, the former spouse can transfer the value of the debit to an appropriate pension scheme.

The splitting of pension assets need not be equal, but will in all likelihood tend towards equality. Pension assets may be offset against other assets, depending on the nature of he settlement agreed.

What are the implications, for pensions splitting as opposed to income sharing after retirement? The greatest implication would probably be less income for both parties. This is because if the husband, as the older life annuitant, if all of the fund was available, could receive much higher income to be split with his former spouse. However, if the fund itself was split and then annuities purchased for each party, the lower aged (in this case female) annuitant would receive lower income. However, she would have peace of mind and not be dependant on the former spouse in any way.

The concept of 'earmarking' meant waiting for a share of the ex-spouse's pension on retirement. If he died before retirement, the ex-spouse would get nothing. Pensions splitting is certainly better than earmarking, as is sharing the pension fund and becoming an additional member of an occupational scheme fund.

Bear in mind the State pension for ex-spouses. An ex-wife can rely on her own contribution record as well as her ex-husband's, but should also look to making Class 3 voluntary contributions, if any shortfall is expected.

25

Pension Mortgages

A pension mortgage is one where the tax-free lump sum arising from the pension plan at retirement is used to repay the mortgage loan outstanding at the date of retirement.

At one time, mortgage providers insisted on a repayment vehicle for interest-only mortgages, no doubt to ensure that they received back their outlay at retirement date. This is no longer as prevalent as in the past, with most mortgage providers leaving their clients to their own repayment devices.

However, using a tax-free pension lump sum as a mortgage repayment investment vehicle can be hugely tax efficient. This is because the pension contributions made to the pension scheme are tax deductible at your highest rates of tax. The pension scheme then grows tax free, and depending on the type of scheme, should return on average 25% of the value of the fund as tax-free cash. This in turn means that the Inland Revenue has part funded the purchase of your private home through the tax system.

The danger in the pensions mortgage scheme lay in the fact that the lump sum would not be available to boost retirement income, or reduce debt-traditional methods or usages for the tax-free cash. However, on the other hand, the mortgage would be paid off, thus reducing cash outflows after retirement.

Problems have arisen in the past with Inland Revenue funding limits. Individual's earnings have been unable to sustain the levels of funding required to generate the right amount of tax-free cash required to pay off the entire mortgage, and this may have lead to a shortfall. In addition, the mortgage lender could not enforce the use of the tax-free cash to redeem the mortgage (as it could not take a pension scheme as security), and the use of pension mortgages has largely fallen away.

On the bright side, the pension mortgage did ensure that many people, as homeowners, also had substantial additional pension funds, if they decided not to use their tax-free cash to redeem the mortgage loan, but rather to use it for increased retirement income.

26

Pensions Mis-selling – What to Do

Pensions mis-selling first came to prominence following Robert Maxwell's misuse of his company pension schemes to fund his business arrangements. Greater scrutiny of all pension funds resulted, and investigations were made into those employees who had transferred out of perfectly good company final salary pension schemes into personal pension plans, mostly to their detriment.

The practice to contract out of SERPS was fuelled by the Government which offered what was essentially a 'bribe' to leave the SERPS (State Earnings Related Pension Scheme) by allowing companies and other employers to pay less in National Insurance to the State by having NI contributions paid into appropriate pension plans for employees contracting out of SERPS. Whilst the contracted out amounts were much higher previously, even today, in 2002/03, employees pay 10% NICs where contracted in and 8.4% where the scheme is contracted out (on earnings between £89.00 and £585 per week); whereas employers' contributions over £89 per week are 11.8% where contracted in and 8.3% where contracted out (final salary schemes) and 11.8% on contracted out money purchase arrangements.

The bottom line is that it would not normally be beneficial to contract out or leave an occupational pension scheme when both employer and employer contribute to leave it for one where only the employee is contributing.

At one stage, statistics put forward by life offices favoured better returns through contracting out, but then, after a few years, others brought out statistics stating that those who had contracted out may be better off if they now contracted back into SERPS. This was particularly the case for older ages. However, in the interim, life offices were fuelling the contracting out process, and financial advisers were moving employees from final salary and other occupational pensions schemes into personal pension schemes where high commissions were payable, thus further depleting the value of pension funds. During this time, transfer values of pension schemes were also penalised meaning lower values eventuated for the transferee.

A financial services industry outcry followed and the Securities and Investments Board (now the FSA) initiated a lengthy pensions review process to uncover pension mis-selling. The review process has found that many people were wrongly advised to contract out of their employers' pension schemes and could be re-instated according to the rules that originally applied to them.

If compensation was received for the wrong advice, then the compensation paid was tax free. Employees could also exceed the 15% limit to make up lost contributions, but the excess over the 15% limit would not receive tax relief. Tax reliefs may be retained by paying back-contributions by instalments.

Pensions providers and financial adviser firms have been through pension review processes for some years now, and it is unlikely that many of those eligible for compensation or re-instatement have not been contacted to do so.

If any reader has been moved from an employer's pension scheme to a personal pension plan, then contact the product provider of the personal pension scheme to make enquiries as to whether the advice given to do so was correctly given. Failing an adequate response, contact the Financial Services Authority (FSA) on 0845 606 1234, which is their consumer helpline number.

Being wrongly advised to move from an employer's occupational pension scheme into an unsuitable personal pension arrangement is one thing. To properly retire from an occupational pension scheme is another. The two must not be confused. It may be that at retirement, a better income stream can be achieved for you by moving your funds generated by that scheme, to a personal pension scheme to make use of the open market option and other benefits. For example, some occupational pension schemes may not give adequate death benefits, or not allow the class of beneficiary required by the retiree to benefit, after the retiree's death, at the benefit levels that could be obtained elsewhere.

You may have other reasons for leaving an employer's occupational pension scheme, and these may not even be commercial, but important to you. For example, you were made redundant or dismissed from an employer, and do not want to be associated with that former employer under any circumstances – or you have found new employment and joined a new employer's pension scheme, considered better than the one where you were previously. Under those circumstances, it may well be in your personal interests to transfer to the new employer's scheme.

Whatever your personal circumstances, make sure that the numbers are calculated, so that you may be advised properly on your future course of action. Comparisons can then be made and options laid out for you to consider. Hopefully pensions mis-selling is a thing of the past, but one can never be too careful.

27

Building a Suitable Pension Fund

One must decide on your normal retirement date first, then what target pension income in retirement is required. Retirement income need not only come from pension funds, it can arise from income from savings and investments as well. If you have a reasonable expectation of an inheritance, or other windfall, then this aspect may also form part of your planning. However, as the latter can never be a certainty, it is wise to treat it as a 'maybe' rather than firm fact, and then to concentrate on building savings and investments.

Also to be taken into account is the following:

1. **Lump sum disbursements at retirement.** For example, paying off debts, or redeeming a mortgage, buying a new car, taking a well-deserved holiday, paying for university fees and other capital expenditures.

2. **Ongoing outflows of income.** Monthly expenditures, regular payments and providing for exceptional out of ordinary small one-off costs.

3. **Your attitude to risk** will determine what sort of funds you will be investing into. A cautious investor will choose low risk investments, a more speculative investor will choose higher-risk investments, but with prospects of capital growth beyond the norm.

4. **Tax efficiency requirements.** Higher rated taxpayers may require investments that reduce or relieve tax (as may those who pay tax at lower levels).

5. **Surplus income and capital available** for investment purposes. It may be that you intend to sell your house at retirement to generate more capital and move to a cheaper house, at home or abroad.

6. **Your investment objectives.** These would include the need for capital growth or income during the initial pre-retirement investment phase, and then possibly a change in investment structure after retirement to provide greater levels of income when you cease work. Also to be taken into account would be the size of target capital required at retirement, its flexibility and accessibility, and whether for retirement only, or perhaps long term care requirements, provision for dependants and other criteria.

7. **Protection of capital and future retirement funds.** Are the funds required for a single individual, or to pay a pension for a spouse or partner. Is the avoidance of inheritance tax and general loss of capital at death of retirement funds of great importance?

8. **Your work status.** If you are employed, or self-employed, or unemployed will affect the type of pension funding you may be able to make. Different rules apply to different employment categories when funding for a pension, or making additional pension contributions, and there may be Inland Revenue limits on the level of funding allowed. Whereas previously, if you had no relevant earnings (arising from employment or taxable income from certain categories), you could not make a pension plan contribution. Now, under the stakeholder rules, up to £3,600 p.a. gross (£2,808) net may be made by anyone, irrespective of how the income arises.

9. The amount of the **state senior citizen's pension** from age 65.

The above are some of the main factors to be taken into account when deciding on building suitable pension and investment funds. Others may include the fact that some people are distrustful of pensions generally, and do not want to invest in pensions (they fear loss of funds on death, as well as being tied into an annuity purchase at a lower rate for the rest of their lives, and feel they can do better if investing their scarce cash resources elsewhere, with more personal control). Some people may be under the mistaken belief that their employers are taking care of their retirement funding and benefits.

With regard to the two factors mentioned above, there are ways to protect your fund so that you don't lose it on death (which is also inheritance tax effective), and also ways to ensure maximum income from pension funds, even within current strictures. This is the case, even with final salary schemes, that may be poor-performing. Secondly, you must assume responsibility for your own pension funding and do not rely on your employer to ensure your safe and effective retirement. It is up to you, and you alone, to check out your personal situation and to do something about it.

The following table usually excites much interest. You will see what it takes to build a £1 million pension fund, and that the earlier you start, the better.

Contributions required at various ages to have £1 million at age 65

Age	Term Years	Contribution p.a. (p.m.)	Interest 10% Compound p.a.	Value
1	65	£152 (£12.78 pm)	10%	£1m
15	50	£687 (£57.25 pm)	10%	£1m
20	45	£1,265 (£105 pm)	10%	£1m
25	40	£2,055 (£171 pm)	10%	£1m
30	35	£3,355 (£280 pm)	10%	£1m
35	30	£5,530 (£461 pm)	10%	£1m
40	25	£9,250 (£770 pm)	10%	£1m
45	20	£15,900 (£1,325 pm)	10%	£1m
50	15	£28,600 (£2,383 pm)	10%	£1m
55	10	£57,100 (£4,758 pm)	10%	£1m
60	5	£150,000 (£12,500 pm)	10%	£1m

The above assumes no charges, and is shown at one rate of interest (10%) over the term as opposed to the more generally accepted range of 5% or 8%. It also assumes a gross pension contribution at that level, whereas payments are actually made net at 22% tax relief. However, pension tax reliefs may not be around for ever, so the gross return is used. A parent could build a £1million pension fund at age 65 for a child age one now, for less than £13 per month. However, if you are age 40 now then you would need to save £770 per month over the next 25 years for a million pound fund. It will take less time if contributions are tax relievable, or average fund growth exceeds 10% compound per annum.

How much should you be contributing towards retirement income? The minimum is in the region of 10%, but it depends on your age, surplus income, and target fund, and could be as much as 30-40% for much older ages.

Your objective is then to establish exactly what your target funds are going to be. To do this, you must assume a rate of investment growth on your target fund, and also a percentage return of income from the funds, once retirement starts (without eating into capital).

Let us assume you wish to retire at age 65, in 20 years' time, on a target income of £50,000 gross per annum.

Assume also that to earn £50,000 from your fund per year, at say 5% of fund value, then you will need to have a fund worth at least £1 million.

[£1 million x 5% = £50,000]

From the table above, you would need to save £1,325 per month to achieve your target income.

The examples that follow will give you an idea of what is involved in building a retirement plan, if employed or self employed.

Example 1

Tom is married and employed by GasElectronics PLC as a middle manager. He is age 45 now. The company operates a final salary scheme. Tom will have 30 years service with the company and can expect a pension based on 30/60ths of his final salary. He will also receive a tax-free lump sum at retirement of 1.5 times his annual pension. Tom is presently earning £28,000 p.a. and his final salary at age 65 is expected to be £50,571(compounded at 3% to age 65). His target income is £50,000 per annum in retirement.

From Employer Pension:	30/60 (50%) x £50 571 =	£25,286
From tax-free lump sum:	£37,929 x 5% income =	£1,896
From State Pension:	£10,885 at age 65 =	£10,885
(£115.9 pw compounded at 2.5% to age 65, using 2001/02 figures)		
Total:		**£38 067**
Shortfall:	(£50,000 – £38,067) =	(£11,993)
Total:		**£50,000**

Investment lump sum required: £119,930 at 10%; £239,860 at 5% investment growth to give income of £11,993 at age 65.

Investment solution:

1. Contribute maximum to stakeholder pension (£3,600 gross or £2,808 net) p.a. Tom is employed, but his present earnings are under £30,000 p.a., so he can contribute to a stakeholder personal pension plan.
2. Contribute 15% of salary to additional voluntary contributions (AVC or FSAVC). This would be £4,200 p.a.
3. Make investments from surplus income.

Taking the worst scenario, Tom would have to plan to fund for, say, £240,000 over the next 20 years. He would have to fund £10,986 per annum for 20 years at 10% or £11,484 p.a. if growth was 5%.

To Fund p.a. (say)		£11,000
Stakeholder (for now)	£3,600	
AVC	£4,200	
Other	£3,200	
Total:		**£11,000**

Example 2

Lavinia is a married self-employed PR consultant. She is age 45 and wishes to retire at age 65. Lavinia has been contributing to Personal Pension Plans for the last 12 years, although she was previously employed, and has a small employer's pension fund from that previous employment, which was a money purchase fund. The value of her pension plans together amounts to £260,000 at this stage. Her net relevant earnings for the tax year are £48,000 for pension contribution purposes. She expects her earnings to rise with inflation. Lavinia wishes to have a target income of £50,000 at age 65.

Income from pension fund at age 65:	£11,700
(based on 75% of fund at 6% return)	
Income from 25% tax-free lump sum:	£6,500
(invested at 10% income age 65)	
State pension at 65:	£10,885
(£115.90 pw increased at 2.5% pa to age 65, using 2001/02 figures)	
Total income: (gross)	£29,085
Shortfall:	£20,915
Total:	**£50,000**

Investment solution

Lavinia has an income shortfall at age 65 of £20,915 p.a. To achieve this income she needs funds of £209,150 invested at 10% and £418,300 invested at 5% growth over the period. A median point would be say £300,000 invested at 7.5% to achieve her income target dependent on her risk profile for investments.

1. She can contribute from age 46 at 25% of her net relevant earnings (or the stakeholder amount of up to £3,600 if this would be more) into personal pension plan funding. This would be 25% x £48,000 = £12,000 p.a. Pension contributions are tax deductible, so the net cost is less 40% tax in total.

2. She can make investments from surplus cash. Some of these may

be tax relievable, thus reducing her net cost.

Lavinia would need to invest £14,041 per annum, with a growth rate of 7.5% compound over the period of 20 years to achieve her investment fund target of £300,000.

From pension contributions:	£12,000
From income surplus:	£2,041
Total:	**£14,041**

Note that 25% of her pension fund would give tax-free cash, so if Lavinia wanted to use part of her funds for tax-free cash investments, she may do so. It has been assumed that the return from the pension fund and returns from tax-free cash are the same. Note that investment returns should be monitored and if long-term averages are below those expected, then greater funding levels are required.

Building a suitable pension fund therefore requires a calculation taking into account your target income at retirement age. One has to work backwards from this position, taking into account existing funds and their projected returns, from all sources. Do not make the fatal mistake of believing your pension fund will get you to your target income alone. If on a '60ths' fund, for example, you will need 30 years of unbroken service with the same employer to achieve 50% of your salary at retirement. In Tom's case, he needed to invest 11,000/28,000 or 40% of his income to achieve his target. In Lavinia's case, she needed to invest 14,041/48,000 or nearly 30% of her income currently to achieve her target.

The message is clear – the younger you start, the less there is to make up at the end of the process. It is possible to build significant retirement funds if committed and dedicated to the process. Not all of these need to be in pension funding; savings and investments from all sources will be useful adjuncts.

28

Retiring Abroad

Many retirees, sick of British winters, seek warmer climes for their retirement years, or to be near family, or for many other reasons. Currently, the older you get, the greater the chance of something medically going wrong with you, and the need for quick and speedy medical attention. France, Germany and Belgium have been popular destinations for those wanting rapid medical treatment and higher standards of care, and no doubt these considerations feature in the retirement plans of many.

Wherever your retirement destination, how you manage your financial affairs and money is going to be an important consideration. For example, should you purchase that flat in Spain, owing it directly, or through an offshore company? Passing shares in the company to heirs and dependants could be more tax efficient than passing property in other countries.

Whether you should take your investments with you, and invest them in the new country of residence, or leave them in the UK, or maybe transfer them to an offshore tax haven, make use of trusts to stream income and protect capital, and a host of other considerations need to be taken into account.

Then there are the personal considerations. Will you meet new friends? Should you take a car with you, or buy one there? What if you don't like where you are going and want to come back? Do you keep your investment and tax shelter positions, or do you change them.

The only certainty about life is that it will be subject to change, and one must be prepared to make the necessary adjustments accordingly.

Depending on where you retire to, will determine how your money should be invested, and on what basis. For example, if you lived in the UK all your life and then retired abroad, then ordinarily your residency status and possibly your domicile will change. Residency and domicile are important concepts for tax and inheritance tax reasons. You may have decided to live in Spain (so you are now ordinarily resident in Spain), but decide to be buried in the UK if you die, making your domicile still the UK. That means wherever your assets are in the world, they will be subject to UK inheritance tax. So residency and domicile planning will be important to you.

If you are resident, ordinarily resident and domiciled in the UK, then all of your investment income is taxable in the UK. If you are resident and ordinarily resident, but not UK domiciled, then offshore income arising will only be taxed in the UK if you bring it in to the UK. If you are not resident or ordinarily resident, and no matter what your domicile is, then investment income is not taxed in the UK.

Planning requires great care so as not to be subject to anti-avoidance tax legislation. The best solution would be to have income producing assets in a low-tax country (or offshore tax haven), received by you in such a way as to pay as little tax as possible. In addition, for capital growth to accrue tax free and not be subject to estate or inheritance taxes.

You may require new wills for your assets. Some people have a will for the new country of residence/domicile and assets situated there, and another will for UK assets, for example.

Retiring abroad may be a new adventure, but proper planning is most important to avoid elephant traps which may be waiting for you. The general trend if becoming non-resident and non-domiciled, is to invest offshore and to take income from that source as required. If you can capitalise your income and take irregular capital payments, then so much the better as capital is usually not taxable. People also forget that the UK itself can be a tax haven, and many people invest in the UK's investment structures and portfolios.

Realising assets in the UK may give rise to capital gains tax. If you intend to live abroad for at least 5 years, and sell the assets giving rise to the gains, once you have moved, then no capital gains tax should be payable. If it is payable, capital gains tax is an optional tax and may be deferred under certain circumstances, forever. In other words, it can die with you if properly planned for.

If considering retiring abroad then, undertake a retirement audit with a certified planner specialising in those types of clients. Best advice early on can save much money later, let alone time spent in trying to rectify things.

29

Steps in the Pensions/Retirement Process

With the advent of stakeholder pensions, the first step in the retirement planning process could be when you are born. Children now qualify for a pension scheme, even if they have no earnings. Contributions made also qualify for tax reliefs, even though the individual may not be a taxpayer, as contributions are made 'net'. This means the Inland Revenue pays the basic tax of 22% (2002/03) directly into your plan. Higher rate taxpayers claim an additional 18% through their tax returns.

The totality of what you decide to do will always come down to how much you can afford to contribute to retirement planning to ensure a financially successful retirement. If you start early enough, it may be as little at 10% per annum – if you leave it too late, it could eat up the whole of your pay package. Between these two extremes would be a reasonable funding well within your financial affordability.

The problem is that early working years are where you earn much less than later in life, and have higher costs, especially with mortgages, school fees and other costs that you may not have in later life, when you would be earning at higher levels. The result is that the magic effect of compound interest has a shorter period to run to help build up your funds. It is therefore important to have a simple strategy and to begin planning immediately – no matter at what stage in the retirement planning cycle you happen to be in right now.

The simplest approach is to set a retirement date for normal retirement. For example, you wish to cease working at age 60 or 65, or at least slow down and smell the roses.

Then, you will need to set a target income in retirement. If you believe that all debts (like mortgage, car HP, etc) will be paid off at that date, and that you can manage on a set percentage of your final salary, then that is a starting point. Bear in mind that to set a target income based purely on the maximum pension you may receive, could well leave you short of cash at retirement.

For example, if you worked for the same employer for a maximum of 40 years, the maximum pension to be expected would be 2/3 of your final salary, and if you joined a scheme after 1987 then that could be capped at the pensions cap, currently £97,200 in 2002/03. That means you cannot have a pension from Inland Revenue approved funds of more than 2/3 of £97,200 i.e. £64,800. Schemes prior to 1987 are not subject to the pensions cap. The pensions cap also applies to personal pension plans and money purchase schemes (or defined contribution schemes).

There is a danger of merely taking the Inland Revenue limits as being your maximum levels of retirement income, rather than planning for a true end benefit approach. In other words, how much do I need in retirement, and how am I going to get there?

Retirement planning is not only about pensions. It is also about savings and investments, mitigating taxes, planning for long term care (during retirement) as a possibility, estate planning – making sure there is enough capital in your estate and that your wills are in order, and other areas. It may well include selling the business as a business owner and investing the proceeds, and providing for dependants or a divorced former partner.

Planning also includes making sure that you receive the maximum state pension at age 65, and if you have lived abroad and presently only entitled to a reduced pension, that you consider paying additionally into the state system to increase or maximise your state pension.

The retirement process

1. Pre-earnings phase – usually age 0-18
2. Earnings Phase – usually age 18 to 65. Investment process begins.
3. Retiring phase – can be from age 50 to age 75 (also the annuity and draw-down option phase)
4. Retirement phase – time spent in retirement
5. Long term care – optional phase for 25% of those over age 80
6. Death benefits phase
7. Re-investment for dependants phase

The retirement funding and financial process

Financing phases in sequence	Period	Sequence
Retirement fund and investment accumulation	Working Life	
Retirement countdown with accelerated accumulation of funds	10 yrs before retirement	
Decisions at retirement date for best Income and capital preservation options	At retirement date	
Retirement income and investment management	In retirement	
Providing for long term care from retirement funds if health deteriorates	During retirement	
Asset and income re-distribution providing for dependants and heirs	On death	
Reinvestment for income and capital growth	After death	

More and more people are thinking of retiring early, and with people living longer, you could spend as much time in your retirement, as you did working. At the turn of the 19th century, the average life expectancy of a male was only 49 years, and for a female, 52 years. By the turn of the last century (2000), the average ages had increased to 75 for males and 79 for females. In a hundred years, the life expectancy has nearly doubled. The question is not that we will live forever, but that we will be retired for much longer than ever before. Our own surveys amongst those who have retired indicate that the biggest fear is not so much the fear of a poor investment risk anymore, but more a fear of outliving your capital and therefore your income.

Retirement is a negative perception. We all know it will happen, and some of us even know when, but we still fail to provide for it adequately, because when we were younger, there were always more important purchases to make and money commitments to be borne than to think about retirement planning. As we get older, perhaps we now feel unable to do anything about it, so let life take its course and hope for the best. Sadly, the State will only provide the bare bones of retirement income – for the rest 'if it's to be, it's up to me'.

The bottom line is that each individual must take responsibility for his or her own retirement planning. Don't rely on your employer, or the Government, they are programmed to provide the absolute minimum.

The steps in the retirement process

Step 1
Set a **retirement date** (you don't have to keep to it, or even leave employment at that date, even if you mature your pension schemes). **Retirement date: ....**

Step 2
Set a **target income** for retirement. **Target income: £......... p.a.**

Step 3
Decide if that income will **escalate** or not. Whilst inflation in the

UK is 0.7% as at February 2002 , it has been in double figures in the past (usually 3% or RPI).   **Escalation %:** ....

Step 4

Work out what **average investment growth** can be expected:

........%

(be conservative, possibly at, say, 5% over the next 10-20 years)

Step 5

Establish what **funds will be available** at retirement date: £.........

Step 6

Establish what **income** will be **available from pensions:**   £.........

Step 7

Establish what **income** will be **available from savings and investments** (from the funds in step 5):   £.........

Step 8

Establish what the **state pension** income will be at retirement:

£.........

(in 2002/03 it is £75.50 p.w. for a single person; £120.70 p.w. for a married couple. Increases each September with inflation figure as at April of that year)

Step 9

Work out any **shortfall** between what is expected as target income and actual income [Step 2 minus (Step 6 + Step 7 + Step 8)].

Shortfall in income: £.........

Step 10

Calculate the **size of fund required** to produce the extra income. Assume income is, say, 5% of that fund value per annum.

Size of fund: £.........

Example:

1. Age 65, in 20 years time
2. £50,000 p.a.
3. 3% escalation
4. 5% p.a.
5. £300,000 from tax-free lump sums and sale of house
6. £16,000 p.a. at age 65
7. £15,000 p.a. at 5%
8. £10,885 (current married state pension escalated at 2.5% over 20 years)
9. [£5,000 − (£16,000 + £15,000 + £10,885) = £41,885) = £8,115 p.a.]
10. £162,300 x 5% = £8,115
    (Take £8,115 x 10 = £81,150. Then multiply by 2 = £162,300)

The value of the fund may have to be larger to provide for the escalating income required, or the fund investments will have to provide this additional annual income.

In this case, a fund is required of £162,500 to provide for the shortfall in income of £8,115 p.a. in 20 years time.

Step 11

Decide on how the extra funding will occur. This could be from additional pension fund contributions, or savings and investments from surplus income. It may even bee from the sale of shares or sale of a property, or maturing endowment policy.

Step 12

Break this down to 'bite-size chunks'. The following table will assist you to find the amount that you need to save each month to the target retirement date on a compound interest basis. The assumption is 10% growth net of all charges and taxes. On the table, find the number of years to your retirement and read off the monthly contribution that will yield £10,000 on retirement. All you have to do then is divide the fund by £10,000 and multiply it by the contribution rate.

Amount required to produce £10,000 worth of funds at any given period to retirement date

Years to retirement	Monthly Contribution £
1	798.0
2	380.0
3	241.0
4	172.0
5	130.0
6	103.0
7	84.0
8	69.5
9	58.5
10	50.0
11	43.0
12	37.0
13	32.5
14	28.5
15	25.0
16	22.0
17	19.5
18	17.5
19	15.5
20	14.0
21	12.5
22	11.0
23	10.0
24	9.0
25	8.0
26	7.5
27	6.5
28	6.0
29	5.5
30	5.0
31	4.5
32	4.0
33	3.7
34	3.3

Example

The fund required was £162,500.
Divide by £10,000 = £16
Multiply by the factor for 20 years (in this case), which is £14
£16 x £14 = £224 needs to be saved each month to reach the fund
target of £162,500 over 20 years time.

At retirement

At retirement, there are again a number of steps in the process. In fact, many of these steps should be taken in the 6-12 months at least before retirement, so that you have taken the necessary actions prior to the actual retirement date.

Step 1

Analyse pension funds. Decide on best retirement route. The choice would be from:

- **If employed** – obtain pension fund details for annual pension, tax-free lump sum, annual pension escalation, death in service benefits, fund transfer value.

- **If self-employed**, or with personal pension plans, money purchase defined contribution type schemes, then you have a number of options, such as:
  i) conventional retirement, using annuities or
  ii) phased retirement, using a mixtures of annuities and income draw-down
  iii) income draw-down from existing pension funds to age 75, then to take an annuity.

Decide what sort of pension or annuity or income scheme to have. Is it a single pension, or must it pay out for two lifetimes (you and your spouse or partner)? Do you want guarantees? Must it pay out a pension or annuity monthly in arrear or advance, or quarterly, six-monthly or annually? Do you wish for your funds to be capital protected? This means that the balance of your funds (or more) is returned to your estate on death, or in trust for your heirs and dependants, free of all taxes. On your death, do you want a 50% pension for the survivor, or a 2/3 pension?

Step 2

Consolidate pension funds, and check transfer values against the best available open market option (best rate from best annuity provider).

If in an occupational pension scheme, it may also pay you to shop around. Obtain a transfer value from your pension scheme. You could do better than what is being offered from the occupational pension scheme. However, if you do decide to transfer for a better deal, make sure death benefits, pension escalations and other benefits are comparable. Some people transfer from occupational pension schemes to obtain better dependants' benefits for example.

Step 3

Check the basis of **death benefits payable** by pension funds. The worst type could be 'return of premiums plus, say, 4% or 5%', whereas a return of fund value is better. You can get the product provider to change the basis of death benefits on application, but there may be a fee charged for doing so.

Step 4

Check for **annuity guarantees** written into the policy documentation. Some product providers could guarantee to pay at a rate of 14% or more, and you may lose out by transferring the fund, even under the open market option.

Step 5

If a **smoker or medically challenged**, get yourself underwritten for an 'impaired life' annuity rate. You could significantly increase your income in this way. If in an occupational pension scheme, the reverse could happen. Because of your medical condition, you may have to take early retirement, and would be penalised, receiving less pension. If the fund was transferred to an impaired life underwriter, you could significantly increase your pension income, depending on your condition, although other factors, such as the pensions cap, could be a limiting factor.

Step 6

Determine your **investment risk and strategy** at retirement. Is it the same as before retirement date? Are you now more cautious with your money, because you have stopped work, with less income or none coming in from other sources? Should you adopt a higher risk profile on some of your capital for prospective increased returns?

Step 7

Examine your existing investment portfolio closely to see that it meets with your objectives. Also determine how your tax-free cash lump sums will be invested. Are the investments required as part of your income objectives, or merely for additional capital growth?

Step 8

Reduce or eliminate as much debt at retirement as is possible.

Step 9

You may need to replace lost life cover, particularly if death in service benefits ended at retirement. This should be done in expectation of retirement, and as early as possible. The younger you are, the cheaper it is. Some retirement schemes protect retirement pension capital with life policy guarantees, and this may be an opportunity to increase life cover if required. If adequately funded and with no liabilities or inheritance taxes, you would need less life cover.

Step 10
>Once your objectives have been established, and you have consolidated your retirement position, you can take various actions to physically retire. You will have made your choices and taken your options, some of them irrevocable. It is now time to 'smell the roses' and to enjoy your retirement years.

How to get help

There is a lot to do prior to retirement, and you must be certain that you are on the right track. Mistakes could be costly. You may need someone to give your retirement plan the 'once over', or have a financial planner give you guidance. Be prepared to pay a fee for this. You could also ask Retirement Strategies Limited (01743 356161) for a retirement planning workstation and workbook to take you through an extensive check list regarding all of your financial planning, which means there is a lot you can do yourself before incurring too much in costs.

During retirement

The main steps to be taken during retirement will be to monitor your investment portfolios, and to make changes where necessary. There will also be decisions to be made regarding pension policies maturing at different dates, further investment of tax-free lump sums , as well as annuity purchases from time to time.

You may also have to provide for long term care, sometimes residential, at other times incorporating frail care with medical facilities, as part of your later retirement strategy. This may require you to have specific types of investments that protect your assets should you have to go into care. For example, if the State pays, it could dispossess your house at a later date. You can protect against this, if it arises, but planning is required.

In addition, retirement is not only about the money. You may have personal development plans to keep yourself active, and developing other interests may be important to your well-being.

If a spouse or partner dies

If death occurs during retirement, then this is traumatic enough, without having to worry about sufficient income and capital for those left behind. Ensure that your wills are up to date and that your personal financial affairs are in order at all times. Life policies underwritten in trust are useful because the proceeds are payable directly to beneficiaries through the trust, without having to wait for probate, which could be a blocker on funds required from the estate. Check also your existing policies to see if they are underwritten in trust or not, so that the appropriate steps may be taken before the event occurs to ensure the proceeds are directed to where you want them to go.

Planning for retirement and the steps in the process given above are not conclusive. What has been given is a broad brush approach to get you on track. Everyone's circumstances are different and the steps in their individual processes will differ accordingly. If you have an action plan and a strategy with a check list, then you can keep yourself on track.

30

Who Can Help You with Pensions Questions?

You may have technical queries requiring answers, or retirement planning questions that need answering. Obviously your first port of call will be your pensions advisers and financial planners, and if you do not have one, then call the authors' advice lines on either 01743 358 480 or 01579 346160, where you will be pointed in the right direction.

Retirement planning countdown seminars are held regularly and there is literature on many topics provided by product providers as well as from one of the many annuity services available to assist you with your retirement and pensions planning.

Epilogue

Pensions Simplified as a book was written to satisfy the needs of ordinary people looking for simple answers to the myriad pensions and retirement planning questions and strategies that need to be taken into account to ensure a successful and financially independent retirement. Generally speaking, books on the subject tend to be either highly technical with few practical answers, or too general in nature. For example, you may be advised that if you haven't prepared well enough for sufficient income in retirement, to only eat two meals a day and move to a smaller house as being the answer to not having enough pension funding in place! Investments should be safe, meaning in the building society or bank, and be prepared to lose your retirement capital from pension funds to the product providers when you die.

In reality, this type of solution benefits no one. There has been no planning to speak of, and the result is seen as fatalistic. The alternative would be set objectives for retirement, to plan the result of your endeavours, to get the best income possible, to ensure that you have capital growth for the longer term, and to protect your fund capital, as well as your heirs and dependants.

Currently, the debate centres on pension funds ultimately providing an income through annuities. You may take income until age 75, but then you must purchase an annuity. This is true certainly of personal pension, retirement annuities and similar plans, and most final salary schemes, which are annuity based. If general investment performance is poor, and interest rates in the economy are low, then annuity rates will suffer. The current annuity product architects are trying to find ways to make an annuity perform better to provide more income from your funds. However, this may be adding additional risk to your income streams (if a unit linked or with profits annuity, or whatever). In fact the annuity problem can be largely overcome, even where there are declining interest rates, through other means, such as medically underwriting annuitants for higher annuities, taking guarantees away from the annuity itself (guarantees could cost up to 70% of the value of your funds), and rather insuring the fund, and other mechanisms.

Many people are worried that their pension funds are not protected in retirement from dying too soon. They have cause to be worried. Traditionally annuity providers take the surplus funds on death of the annuitant. However, in some countries, annuity surpluses are paid to the estate of the deceased annuitant, and the UK is seeing the first annuity products promising to do just that. However, there has been no general statement from the pensions product providers on this iniquitous issue to date, and rather than have the cost of insuring your fund to return capital, there should be a mechanism whereby the product provider does so. This should also apply to final salary schemes and similar funds.

Pensions Simplified has also focused on the different types of pension plans available and when to use them. A core development in the pensions industry, following the regulator's and journalists' endeavours in this area has been the simplification of pension funds and their investment components and charging structures. This has lead to a decrease in pension funds' cost structures, and greater value for money when taking out new pension funds. Many product providers are working within the 1% cost structure prescribed for stakeholder pensions, for all their funds, and the consumer pensions purchaser is the winner.

Whilst the pensions legislation remains complicated, pensions products are becoming easier to understand and simple in their construction. They are also becoming cheaper, thus shifting the direction from commission-based advice towards fee-based retirement planning in general.

Financial planners have a great responsibility to ensure that their clients not only get the best deal for retirement, but are adequately prepared for their retirement journeys and for what lies beyond. However, the challenge is equally that of the client, to ensure that the advice he or she receives is adequate, and that mistakes are not made in the preparation process.

Pensions Simplified should go a long way to assist those planning for retirement by explaining in easy to understand terms, the various processes involved.

Tony Granger and Richard Bateman
Shrewsbury and Liskeard

Abbreviations

ADLs   Activities of Daily Living
AEI   Average Earnings Index
AVC   Additional Voluntary Contributions scheme
CAT   Charges, Access, Terms
CFP   Certified Financial Planner
COMPS   Contracted Out Money Purchase Scheme
COSR   Contracted Out Salary Related Scheme
DB   Defined Benefits – occupational pension scheme
DC   Defined Contribution – occupational and other pension scheme
EBT   Employee Benefit Trust
EPP   Executive Pension Plan
FSA   Financial Services Authority
FSAVC   Free Standing Additional Voluntary Contribution scheme
FURBS   Funded Unapproved Retirement Benefit Scheme
GMP   Guaranteed Minimum Pension
GPPP   Group Personal Pensions Plan
HP   Hire Purchase
IPA   Individual Pension Account
ISA   Individual Savings Account
LEL   Lower Earnings Limit
LIA   Life Assurance Association
MFR   Minimum Funding Requirement
MP   Money Purchase
NI   National Insurance
NRE   Net relevant Earnings
OEIC ·   Open Ended Investment Plan
OMO   Open Market Option
PA   Per Annum
PIPPA   Plan where pension fund is insured
PPP   Personal Pension Plan

PW	Per Week
RA	Retirement Annuity
RPI	Retail Prices Index
SERPS	State Earnings Related Pension Scheme
S2P	State Second Pension
SIPP	Self-Invested Personal Pension plan
SOFA	Society of Financial Advisers
SPP	Stakeholder Pension Plan
SSAS	Small Self Administered Scheme
TA	Taxes Act 1988
TFC	Tax-free Cash
UURBS	Unfunded Unapproved Retirement Benefit Scheme
VCT	Venture Capital Trust

Index

For further confidential information on pensions options, send this page to:

**Retirement Strategies
Allinson House
Oxon Business Park
Shrewsbury
SY3 5HJ**

Name _____

Address

_____

_____

_____

_____ Postcode _____

Telephone: _____

Fax: _____

Email: _____

I would like further information on the following (please state your requirements):

Post to the address above, fax to 01743 358481, or email to
info@mentorcorporation.co.uk

Please photocopy thie page to avoid spoiling your book